T0085800

THIS BOOK BELONGS TO:

TRACKING MY LIFE

Chart Your
Progress
and Celebrate
Wins
Every Day

NICOLE BARLETTANO

A TarcherPerigee Book

An imprint of Penguin Random House LLC
penguinrandomhouse.com

Copyright © 2023 by Nicole Barlettano
Penguin Random House supports copyright. Copyright fuels creativity,
encourages diverse voices, promotes free speech, and creates a vibrant
culture. Thank you for buying an authorized edition of this book and for
complying with copyright laws by not reproducing, scanning, or distributing
any part of it in any form without permission. You are supporting writers
and allowing Penguin Random House to continue to publish books for every
reader.

TarcherPerigee with tp colophon is a registered trademark of Penguin Random
House LLC.

Most TarcherPerigee books are available at special quantity discounts for
bulk purchase for sales promotions, premiums, fund-raising, and educational
needs. Special books or book excerpts also can be created to fit specific needs.
For details, write SpecialMarkets@penguinrandomhouse.com.

Trade paperback ISBN: 9780593543122
Library of Congress Control Number: 2022946764

Printed in the United States of America
1st Printing

Book design by Nicole Barlettano

Neither the publisher nor the author is engaged in rendering professional
advice or services to the individual reader. The ideas, procedures, and
suggestions contained in this book are not intended as a substitute for
consulting with your physician. All matters regarding your health require
medical supervision. Neither the author nor the publisher shall be liable or
responsible for any loss or damage allegedly arising from any information
or suggestion in this book.

THIS IS FOR YOU, MOM.
THANKS FOR ALWAYS KEEPING
ME ON TRACK
143

CONTENTS

HOUSEHOLD

FINANCIAL

MENTAL HEALTH

SELF-CARE

PRODUCTIVITY

TRACKING MY LIFE

INTRODUCTION

WELCOME TO <u>TRACKING MY LIFE</u>, A GUIDED JOURNAL FULL OF EVERYDAY PAGES TO TRACK YOUR PROGRESS AND CELEBRATE YOUR WINS!

TAKE SOME TIME TO QUIET THE CHAOS AND TRACK ALL AREAS OF YOUR LIFE. YOU'LL FIND THAT TRACKING GIVES YOU A SENSE OF ACCOMPLISHMENT, HELPS WITH MEMORY KEEPING, SUPPORTS SELF-DISCOVERY, AND SERVES AS A GREAT TOOL TO HELP YOU REACH GOALS YOU ONCE THOUGHT UNATTAINABLE.

EACH PAGE IS FILLED WITH FUN AND FUNCTIONAL TRACKING TOOLS TO HELP YOU IMPROVE YOUR LIFE AND ACKNOWLEDGE YOUR PROGRESS. DON'T FORGET TO HAVE FUN WITH IT! ONCE YOU ACCOMPLISH A GOAL, ADD SOME COLOR AND GET CREATIVE!

YOU CAN NAVIGATE THIS BOOK FROM THE FIRST PAGE TO THE LAST, OR YOU CAN SKIP AROUND AND FIND THE TRACKERS THAT WORK FOR YOU RIGHT NOW.

LET'S TAKE A MOMENT TO PAUSE. BE PRESENT. TAKE A BREATH. ARE YOU READY TO BEGIN? LET'S TRACK YOUR LIFE!

✓	TITLE	AUTHOR

BOOKS TO READ

100 DAYS OF READING

TAKE TIME TO READ EACH DAY, AND RECORD IT!

☆ _____ ☆ _____
☆ _____ ☆ _____
☆ _____ ☆ _____
☆ _____ ☆ _____
☆ _____ ☆ _____
☆ _____ ☆ _____
☆ _____ ☆ _____
☆ _____ ☆ _____
☆ _____ ☆ _____
☆ _____ ☆ _____
☆ _____ ☆ _____
☆ _____ ☆ _____
☆ _____ ☆ _____
☆ _____ ☆ _____
☆ _____ ☆ _____
☆ _____ ☆ _____
☆ _____ ☆ _____

TICKETS

☆ MOVIES TO WATCH ☆

TV TO WATCH

SHOW:

SHOW:

SHOW:

SHOW:

SHOW:

SHOW:

SHOW:

SHOW:

SHOW:

SHOW:

SHOW:

SHOW:

BUILD YOUR SOUNDTRACK

IS YOUR LIFE'S PLAYLIST FUNKY AND FUN OR SMOOTH AND RELAXING?
BUILD THE SOUNDTRACK TO YOUR LIFE!

SONG:

ARTIST:

_____   _____
_____   _____
_____   _____
_____   _____
_____   _____
_____   _____
_____   _____
_____   _____
_____   _____
_____   _____
_____   _____
_____   _____
_____   _____
_____   _____
_____   _____
_____   _____
_____   _____
_____   _____

PODCASTS TO LISTEN TO

PODCAST: _____
EPISODES: _____
_____
_____
RATING: ☆ ☆ ☆ ☆ ☆

PODCAST: _____
EPISODES: _____
_____
_____
RATING: ☆ ☆ ☆ ☆ ☆

PODCAST: _____
EPISODES: _____
_____
_____
RATING: ☆ ☆ ☆ ☆ ☆

PODCAST: _____
EPISODES: _____
_____
_____
RATING: ☆ ☆ ☆ ☆ ☆

PODCAST: _____
EPISODES: _____
_____
_____
RATING: ☆ ☆ ☆ ☆ ☆

PODCAST: _____
EPISODES: _____
_____
_____
RATING: ☆ ☆ ☆ ☆ ☆

PODCAST: _____
EPISODES: _____
_____
_____
RATING: ☆ ☆ ☆ ☆ ☆

PODCAST: _____
EPISODES: _____
_____
_____
RATING: ☆ ☆ ☆ ☆ ☆

VIDEO GAMES TO PLAY

SO MANY GAMES, SO LITTLE TIME! KEEP TRACK OF THE GAMES YOU WANT TO PLAY!

GAME: _____
SYSTEM: _____
NOTES: _____
_____
_____

GAME: _____
SYSTEM: _____
NOTES: _____
_____
_____

GAME: _____
SYSTEM: _____
NOTES: _____
_____
_____

GAME: _____
SYSTEM: _____
NOTES: _____
_____
_____

GAME: _____
SYSTEM: _____
NOTES: _____
_____
_____

GAME: _____
SYSTEM: _____
NOTES: _____
_____
_____

GAME: _____
SYSTEM: _____
NOTES: _____
_____
_____

GAME: _____
SYSTEM: _____
NOTES: _____
_____
_____

GAME: _____
SYSTEM: _____
NOTES: _____
_____
_____

GAME: _____
SYSTEM: _____
NOTES: _____
_____
_____

DRINKS I WANT TO TRY

RECORD THE DRINKS YOU'D LIKE TO TRY ON THE GLASSES.
ONCE YOU TRY A NEW DRINK, COLOR IN THE GLASS!

FOODS I WANT TO TRY

RECORD THE FOODS YOU'D LIKE TO TRY ON THE PLATES.
ONCE YOU TRY A NEW FOOD, COLOR IN THE PLATE!

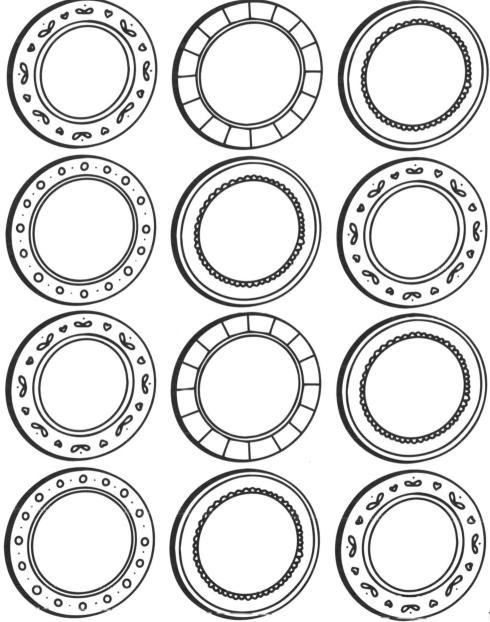

FAVORITE QUOTES

KEEP ALL YOUR FAVORITE QUOTES IN ONE PLACE—FILL IN THE BUBBLES!

12

13

HAPPY MAIL TRACKER

LOVE RECEIVING GOOD OLD-FASHIONED MAIL FROM A PAL? KEEP TRACK OF YOUR CORRESPONDENCE!

TO: _____
FROM: _____
DATE: _____
HIGHLIGHTS: _____
_____
_____

TO: _____
FROM: _____
DATE: _____
HIGHLIGHTS: _____
_____
_____

TO: _____
FROM: _____
DATE: _____
HIGHLIGHTS: _____
_____
_____

TO: _____
FROM: _____
DATE: _____
HIGHLIGHTS: _____
_____
_____

TO: _____
FROM: _____
DATE: _____
HIGHLIGHTS: _____
_____
_____

TO: _____
FROM: _____
DATE: _____
HIGHLIGHTS: _____
_____
_____

TO: _____
FROM: _____
DATE: _____
HIGHLIGHTS: _____
_____
_____

TO: _____
FROM: _____
DATE: _____
HIGHLIGHTS: _____
_____
_____

TO: _____
FROM: _____
DATE: _____
HIGHLIGHTS: _____
_____
_____

TO: _____
FROM: _____
DATE: _____
HIGHLIGHTS: _____
_____
_____

TO: _____
FROM: _____
DATE: _____
HIGHLIGHTS: _____
_____
_____

TO: _____
FROM: _____
DATE: _____
HIGHLIGHTS: _____
_____
_____

TO: _____
FROM: _____
DATE: _____
HIGHLIGHTS: _____
_____
_____

TO: _____
FROM: _____
DATE: _____
HIGHLIGHTS: _____
_____
_____

MY SEARCH HISTORY

KEEP TRACK OF YOUR UNIQUE SEARCH HISTORY!

MY WISHLIST

WHAT'S ON YOUR WISHLIST? KEEP TRACK!

ITEM:	STORE:	PRICE:

GIFT TRACKER

IN A GIVING MOOD? KEEP TRACK OF THE GIFTS YOU GIVE!

PERSON:	GIFT:	PRICE:	✓
_____	_____	_____	☐
_____	_____	_____	☐
_____	_____	_____	☐
_____	_____	_____	☐
_____	_____	_____	☐
_____	_____	_____	☐
_____	_____	_____	☐
_____	_____	_____	☐
_____	_____	_____	☐
_____	_____	_____	☐
_____	_____	_____	☐
_____	_____	_____	☐
_____	_____	_____	☐
_____	_____	_____	☐
_____	_____	_____	☐
_____	_____	_____	☐
_____	_____	_____	☐
_____	_____	_____	☐
_____	_____	_____	☐
_____	_____	_____	☐
_____	_____	_____	☐
_____	_____	_____	☐
_____	_____	_____	☐
_____	_____	_____	☐

GIFTS I'VE RECEIVED

KEEP TRACK OF THOSE NIFTY GIFTIES FROM FRIENDS AND FAMILY!

GIFT: _____
FROM: _____
REASON: _____
THANK-YOU CARD: Ⓨ Ⓝ
NOTES: _____
_____

GIFT: _____
FROM: _____
REASON: _____
THANK-YOU CARD: Ⓨ Ⓝ
NOTES: _____
_____

GIFT: _____
FROM: _____
REASON: _____
THANK-YOU CARD: Ⓨ Ⓝ
NOTES: _____
_____

GIFT: _____
FROM: _____
REASON: _____
THANK-YOU CARD: Ⓨ Ⓝ
NOTES: _____
_____

GIFT: _____
FROM: _____
REASON: _____
THANK-YOU CARD: Ⓨ Ⓝ
NOTES: _____
_____

GIFT: _____
FROM: _____
REASON: _____
THANK-YOU CARD: Ⓨ Ⓝ
NOTES: _____
_____

GIFT: _____
FROM: _____
REASON: _____
THANK-YOU CARD: Ⓨ Ⓝ
NOTES: _____
_____

GIFT: _____
FROM: _____
REASON: _____
THANK-YOU CARD: Ⓨ Ⓝ
NOTES: _____
_____

GIFT: _____
FROM: _____
REASON: _____
THANK-YOU CARD: Ⓨ Ⓝ
NOTES: _____
_____

GIFT: _____
FROM: _____
REASON: _____
THANK-YOU CARD: Ⓨ Ⓝ
NOTES: _____
_____

GIFT: _____
FROM: _____
REASON: _____
THANK-YOU CARD: Ⓨ Ⓝ
NOTES: _____
_____

GIFT: _____
FROM: _____
REASON: _____
THANK-YOU CARD: Ⓨ Ⓝ
NOTES: _____
_____

GIFT: _____	GIFT: _____
FROM: _____	FROM: _____
REASON: _____	REASON: _____
THANK-YOU CARD: (Y) (N)	THANK-YOU CARD: (Y) (N)
NOTES: _____	NOTES: _____
_____	_____

GIFT: _____	GIFT: _____
FROM: _____	FROM: _____
REASON: _____	REASON: _____
THANK-YOU CARD: (Y) (N)	THANK-YOU CARD: (Y) (N)
NOTES: _____	NOTES: _____
_____	_____

GIFT: _____	GIFT: _____
FROM: _____	FROM: _____
REASON: _____	REASON: _____
THANK-YOU CARD: (Y) (N)	THANK-YOU CARD: (Y) (N)
NOTES: _____	NOTES: _____
_____	_____

GIFT: _____	GIFT: _____
FROM: _____	FROM: _____
REASON: _____	REASON: _____
THANK-YOU CARD: (Y) (N)	THANK-YOU CARD: (Y) (N)
NOTES: _____	NOTES: _____
_____	_____

GIFT: _____	GIFT: _____
FROM: _____	FROM: _____
REASON: _____	REASON: _____
THANK-YOU CARD: (Y) (N)	THANK-YOU CARD: (Y) (N)
NOTES: _____	NOTES: _____
_____	_____

GIFT: _____	GIFT: _____
FROM: _____	FROM: _____
REASON: _____	REASON: _____
THANK-YOU CARD: (Y) (N)	THANK-YOU CARD: (Y) (N)
NOTES: _____	NOTES: _____
_____	_____

NOTABLE HOROSCOPES

DID TODAY'S HOROSCOPE STRIKE A CHORD? SAVE IT BELOW AND REFLECT ON IT LATER!

DATE: _____
HOROSCOPE: _____
_____
_____
_____
_____

NOTES: _____
_____
_____

DATE: _____
HOROSCOPE: _____
_____
_____
_____
_____

NOTES: _____
_____
_____

DATE: _____
HOROSCOPE: _____
_____
_____
_____
_____

NOTES: _____
_____
_____

DATE: _____
HOROSCOPE: _____
_____
_____
_____
_____

NOTES: _____
_____
_____

DATE: _____
HOROSCOPE: _____
_____
_____
_____
_____

NOTES: _____
_____
_____

DATE: _____
HOROSCOPE: _____
_____
_____
_____
_____

NOTES: _____
_____
_____

DATE: _____
HOROSCOPE: _____
_____
_____
_____
_____
NOTES: _____
_____
_____

DATE: _____
HOROSCOPE: _____
_____
_____
_____
_____
NOTES: _____
_____
_____

DATE: _____
HOROSCOPE: _____
_____
_____
_____
_____
NOTES: _____
_____
_____

DATE: _____
HOROSCOPE: _____
_____
_____
_____
_____
NOTES: _____
_____
_____

DATE: _____
HOROSCOPE: _____
_____
_____
_____
_____
NOTES: _____
_____
_____

DATE: _____
HOROSCOPE: _____
_____
_____
_____
_____
NOTES: _____
_____
_____

DREAM TRACKER

DREAMS GIVE US A WINDOW INTO OUR MINDS. RECORD YOUR MEMORABLE DREAMS!

DATE: _____

DATE: _____

DATE: _____

DATE: _____

DATE: _____

DATE: _____

DATE: _____

DATE: _____

DATE:_____

DATE:_____

DATE:_____

DATE:_____

DATE:_____

DATE:_____

DATE:_____

DATE:_____

TRAVEL TRACKER

WANDERLUST? TRACK YOUR TRAVEL DREAMS!

DESTINATION: _____

PLACES TO SEE: _____

THINGS TO DO: _____

NOTES: _____
_____
_____

DESTINATION: _____

PLACES TO SEE: _____

THINGS TO DO: _____

NOTES: _____
_____
_____

DESTINATION: _____

PLACES TO SEE: _____

THINGS TO DO: _____

NOTES: _____
_____
_____

DESTINATION: _____

PLACES TO SEE: _____

THINGS TO DO: _____

NOTES: _____
_____
_____

DESTINATION: _____

PLACES TO SEE: _____

THINGS TO DO: _____

NOTES: _____
_____
_____

DESTINATION: _____

PLACES TO SEE: _____

THINGS TO DO: _____

NOTES: _____
_____
_____

DESTINATION: _____

PLACES TO SEE: _____

THINGS TO DO: _____

NOTES: _____
_____
_____

DESTINATION: _____

PLACES TO SEE: _____

THINGS TO DO: _____

NOTES: _____
_____
_____

DESTINATION: _____

PLACES TO SEE: _____

THINGS TO DO: _____

NOTES: _____
_____
_____

DESTINATION: _____

PLACES TO SEE: _____

THINGS TO DO: _____

NOTES: _____
_____
_____

DESTINATION: _____

PLACES TO SEE: _____

THINGS TO DO: _____

NOTES: _____
_____
_____

DESTINATION: _____

PLACES TO SEE: _____

THINGS TO DO: _____

NOTES: _____
_____
_____

PACKING FOR A TRIP

GOING SOMEWHERE?
PACK YOUR BAGS AND TRACK YOUR PROGRESS!

100 DAYS OF YOGA

NAMASTE. EACH DAY THAT YOU PRACTICE YOGA, RECORD IT!

YEARLY MOOD TRACKER

FILL OUT THE MOOD KEY, AND COLOR THE CIRCLES TO REPRESENT YOUR DAILY MOOD!

MOODS:

○ _____
○ _____
○ _____
○ _____
○ _____
○ _____
○ _____
○ _____
○ _____
○ _____
○ _____
○ _____

	J	F	M	A	M	J	J	A	S	O	N	D
1	○	○	○	○	○	○	○	○	○	○	○	○
2	○	○	○	○	○	○	○	○	○	○	○	○
3	○	○	○	○	○	○	○	○	○	○	○	○
4	○	○	○	○	○	○	○	○	○	○	○	○
5	○	○	○	○	○	○	○	○	○	○	○	○
6	○	○	○	○	○	○	○	○	○	○	○	○
7	○	○	○	○	○	○	○	○	○	○	○	○
8	○	○	○	○	○	○	○	○	○	○	○	○
9	○	○	○	○	○	○	○	○	○	○	○	○
10	○	○	○	○	○	○	○	○	○	○	○	○
11	○	○	○	○	○	○	○	○	○	○	○	○
12	○	○	○	○	○	○	○	○	○	○	○	○
13	○	○	○	○	○	○	○	○	○	○	○	○
14	○	○	○	○	○	○	○	○	○	○	○	○
15	○	○	○	○	○	○	○	○	○	○	○	○
16	○	○	○	○	○	○	○	○	○	○	○	○
17	○	○	○	○	○	○	○	○	○	○	○	○
18	○	○	○	○	○	○	○	○	○	○	○	○
19	○	○	○	○	○	○	○	○	○	○	○	○
20	○	○	○	○	○	○	○	○	○	○	○	○
21	○	○	○	○	○	○	○	○	○	○	○	○
22	○	○	○	○	○	○	○	○	○	○	○	○
23	○	○	○	○	○	○	○	○	○	○	○	○
24	○	○	○	○	○	○	○	○	○	○	○	○
25	○	○	○	○	○	○	○	○	○	○	○	○
26	○	○	○	○	○	○	○	○	○	○	○	○
27	○	○	○	○	○	○	○	○	○	○	○	○
28	○	○	○	○	○	○	○	○	○	○	○	○
29	○	○	○	○	○	○	○	○	○	○	○	○
30	○		○	○	○	○	○	○	○	○	○	○
31	○		○		○		○	○		○		○

JANUARY MOOD TRACKER

FILL OUT THE KEY, AND COLOR THE DAILY ICON TO REPRESENT YOUR MOOD!

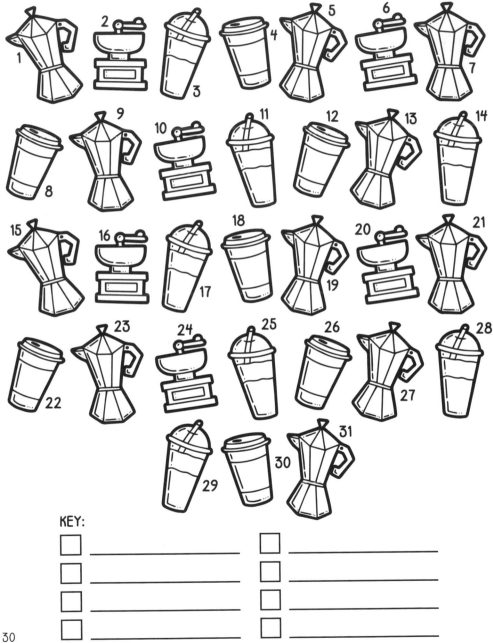

KEY:

☐ _____   ☐ _____
☐ _____   ☐ _____
☐ _____   ☐ _____
☐ _____   ☐ _____

JANUARY GRATITUDE

RECORD 1 LINE OF GRATITUDE EACH DAY!

1 _____
2 _____
3 _____
4 _____
5 _____
6 _____
7 _____
8 _____
9 _____
10 _____
11 _____
12 _____
13 _____
14 _____
15 _____
16 _____
17 _____
18 _____
19 _____
20 _____
21 _____
22 _____
23 _____
24 _____
25 _____
26 _____
27 _____
28 _____
29 _____
30 _____
31 _____

JANUARY MEMORIES

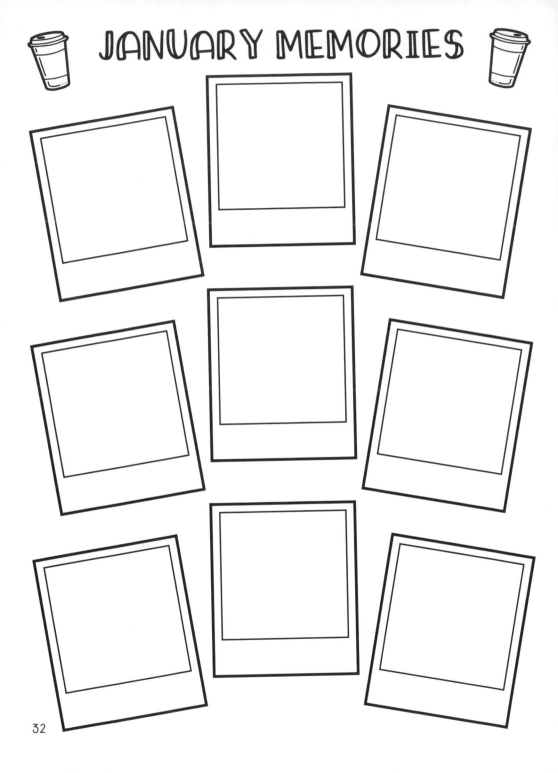

FEBRUARY MOOD TRACKER

FILL OUT THE KEY, AND COLOR THE DAILY ICON TO REPRESENT YOUR MOOD!

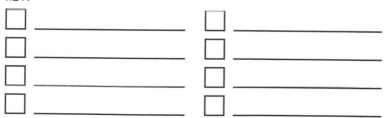

KEY:

FEBRUARY GRATITUDE

RECORD 1 LINE OF GRATITUDE EACH DAY!

1 _____
2 _____
3 _____
4 _____
5 _____
6 _____
7 _____
8 _____
9 _____
10 _____
11 _____
12 _____
13 _____
14 _____
15 _____
16 _____
17 _____
18 _____
19 _____
20 _____
21 _____
22 _____
23 _____
24 _____
25 _____
26 _____
27 _____
28 _____
29 _____

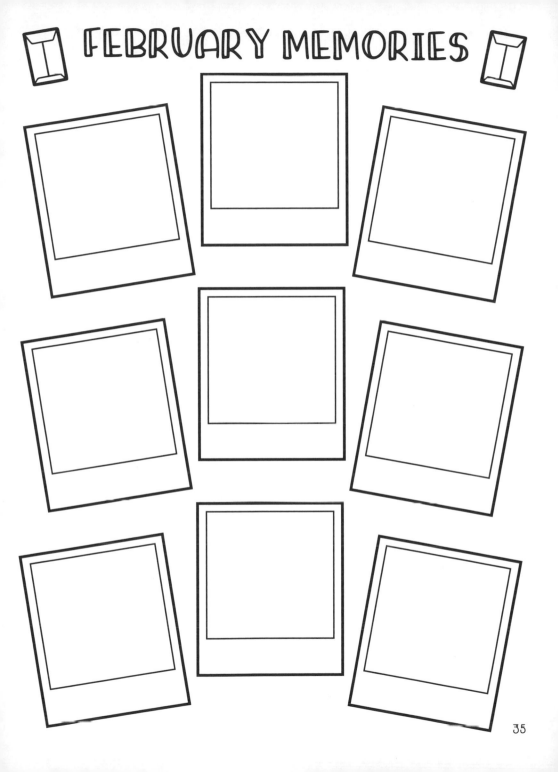

FEBRUARY MEMORIES

35

MARCH MOOD TRACKER

FILL OUT THE KEY, AND COLOR THE DAILY ICON TO REPRESENT YOUR MOOD!

KEY:

☐ _____   ☐ _____

☐ _____   ☐ _____

☐ _____   ☐ _____

☐ _____   ☐ _____

36

MARCH GRATITUDE

RECORD 1 LINE OF GRATITUDE EACH DAY!

1 _____
2 _____
3 _____
4 _____
5 _____
6 _____
7 _____
8 _____
9 _____
10 _____
11 _____
12 _____
13 _____
14 _____
15 _____
16 _____
17 _____
18 _____
19 _____
20 _____
21 _____
22 _____
23 _____
24 _____
25 _____
26 _____
27 _____
28 _____
29 _____
30 _____
31 _____

MARCH MEMORIES

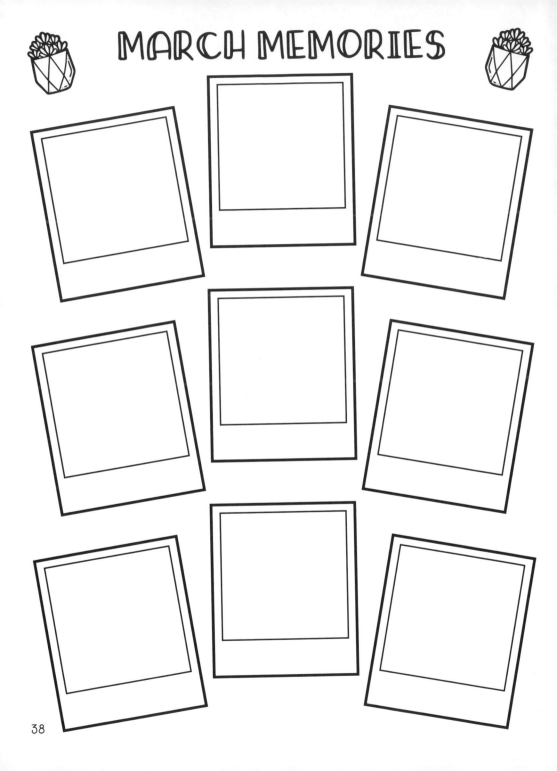

APRIL MOOD TRACKER

FILL OUT THE KEY, AND COLOR THE DAILY ICON TO REPRESENT YOUR MOOD!

 1
 2
 3
 4
 5
 6

 7
 8
 9
 10
 11
 12

 13
 14
 15
 16
 17
 18

 19
 20
 21
 22
 23
 24

 25
 26
 27
 28
 29
 30

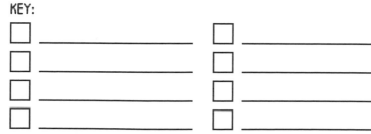

KEY:

☐ _____   ☐ _____

☐ _____   ☐ _____

☐ _____   ☐ _____

☐ _____   ☐ _____

39

APRIL GRATITUDE

RECORD 1 LINE OF GRATITUDE EACH DAY!

1 _____
2 _____
3 _____
4 _____
5 _____
6 _____
7 _____
8 _____
9 _____
10 _____
11 _____
12 _____
13 _____
14 _____
15 _____
16 _____
17 _____
18 _____
19 _____
20 _____
21 _____
22 _____
23 _____
24 _____
25 _____
26 _____
27 _____
28 _____
29 _____
30 _____

APRIL MEMORIES

MAY MOOD TRACKER

FILL OUT THE KEY, AND COLOR THE DAILY ICON TO REPRESENT YOUR MOOD!

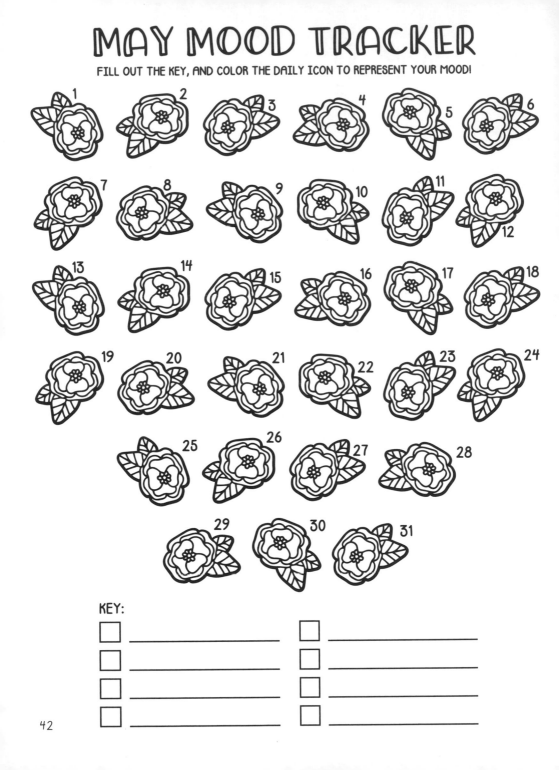

KEY:

☐ _____   ☐ _____

☐ _____   ☐ _____

☐ _____   ☐ _____

☐ _____   ☐ _____

42

MAY GRATITUDE

RECORD 1 LINE OF GRATITUDE EACH DAY!

1 _____
2 _____
3 _____
4 _____
5 _____
6 _____
7 _____
8 _____
9 _____
10 _____
11 _____
12 _____
13 _____
14 _____
15 _____
16 _____
17 _____
18 _____
19 _____
20 _____
21 _____
22 _____
23 _____
24 _____
25 _____
26 _____
27 _____
28 _____
29 _____
30 _____
31 _____

MAY MEMORIES

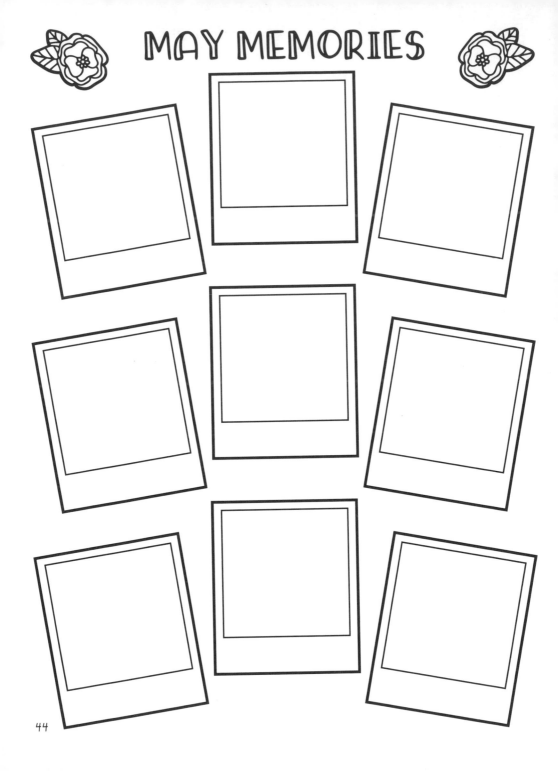

44

JUNE MOOD TRACKER

FILL OUT THE KEY, AND COLOR THE DAILY ICON TO REPRESENT YOUR MOOD!

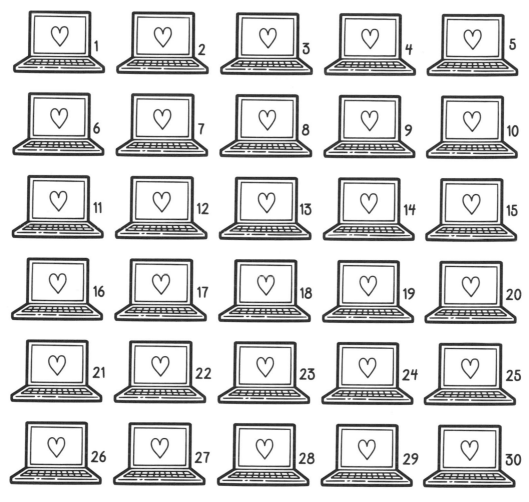

KEY:

☐ _____   ☐ _____
☐ _____   ☐ _____
☐ _____   ☐ _____
☐ _____   ☐ _____

 # JUNE GRATITUDE
RECORD 1 LINE OF GRATITUDE EACH DAY!

1 _____
2 _____
3 _____
4 _____
5 _____
6 _____
7 _____
8 _____
9 _____
10 _____
11 _____
12 _____
13 _____
14 _____
15 _____
16 _____
17 _____
18 _____
19 _____
20 _____
21 _____
22 _____
23 _____
24 _____
25 _____
26 _____
27 _____
28 _____
29 _____
30 _____

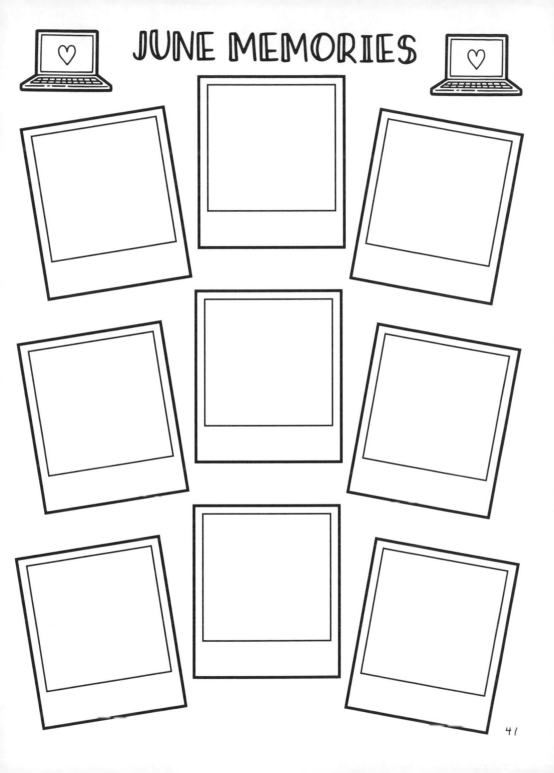

JUNE MEMORIES

41

JULY MOOD TRACKER

FILL OUT THE KEY, AND COLOR THE DAILY ICON TO REPRESENT YOUR MOOD!

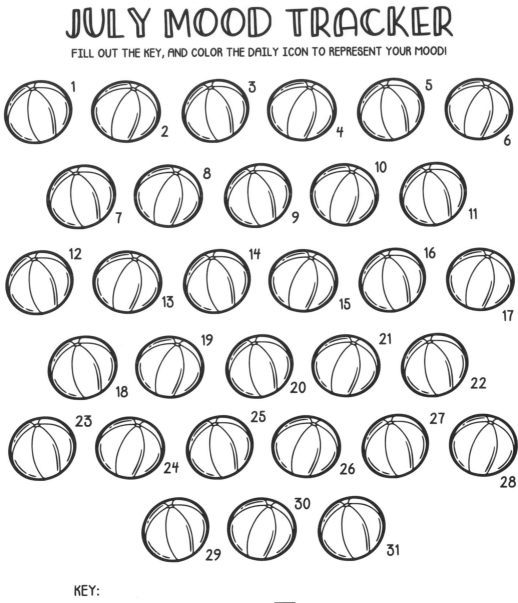

KEY:

☐ _____   ☐ _____
☐ _____   ☐ _____
☐ _____   ☐ _____
☐ _____   ☐ _____

JULY GRATITUDE

RECORD 1 LINE OF GRATITUDE EACH DAY!

1 _____
2 _____
3 _____
4 _____
5 _____
6 _____
7 _____
8 _____
9 _____
10 _____
11 _____
12 _____
13 _____
14 _____
15 _____
16 _____
17 _____
18 _____
19 _____
20 _____
21 _____
22 _____
23 _____
24 _____
25 _____
26 _____
27 _____
28 _____
29 _____
30 _____
31 _____

JULY MEMORIES

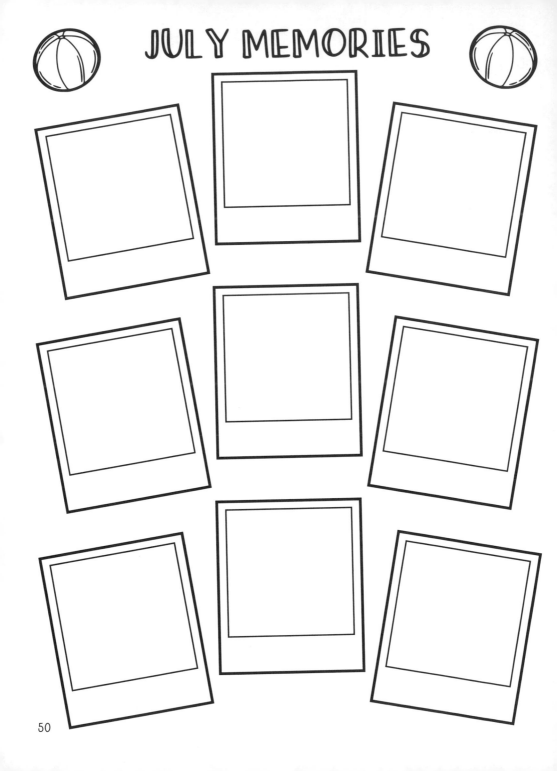

AUGUST MOOD TRACKER

FILL OUT THE KEY, AND COLOR THE DAILY ICON TO REPRESENT YOUR MOOD!

KEY:

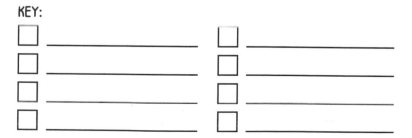

AUGUST GRATITUDE

RECORD 1 LINE OF GRATITUDE EACH DAY!

1 _____
2 _____
3 _____
4 _____
5 _____
6 _____
7 _____
8 _____
9 _____
10 _____
11 _____
12 _____
13 _____
14 _____
15 _____
16 _____
17 _____
18 _____
19 _____
20 _____
21 _____
22 _____
23 _____
24 _____
25 _____
26 _____
27 _____
28 _____
29 _____
30 _____
31 _____

AUGUST MEMORIES

SEPTEMBER MOOD TRACKER

FILL OUT THE KEY, AND COLOR THE DAILY ICON TO REPRESENT YOUR MOOD!

KEY:

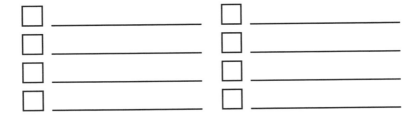

SEPTEMBER GRATITUDE

RECORD 1 LINE OF GRATITUDE EACH DAY!

1 _____
2 _____
3 _____
4 _____
5 _____
6 _____
7 _____
8 _____
9 _____
10 _____
11 _____
12 _____
13 _____
14 _____
15 _____
16 _____
17 _____
18 _____
19 _____
20 _____
21 _____
22 _____
23 _____
24 _____
25 _____
26 _____
27 _____
28 _____
29 _____
30 _____

SEPTEMBER MEMORIES

OCTOBER MOOD TRACKER

FILL OUT THE KEY, AND COLOR THE DAILY ICON TO REPRESENT YOUR MOOD!

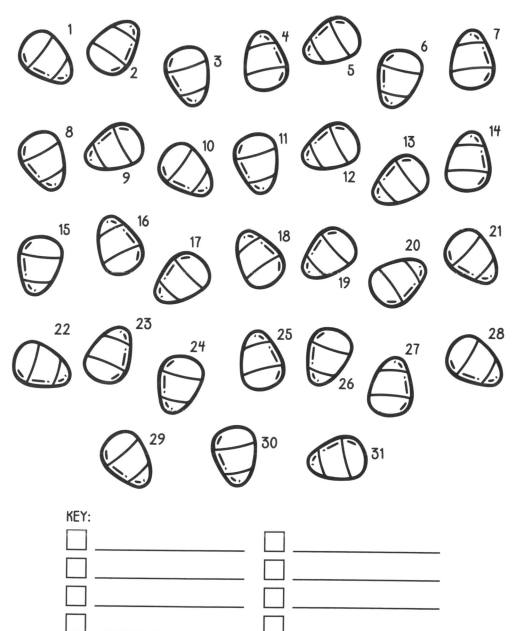

KEY:

☐ _____   ☐ _____
☐ _____   ☐ _____
☐ _____   ☐ _____
☐ _____   ☐ _____

OCTOBER GRATITUDE

RECORD 1 LINE OF GRATITUDE EACH DAY!

1 _____
2 _____
3 _____
4 _____
5 _____
6 _____
7 _____
8 _____
9 _____
10 _____
11 _____
12 _____
13 _____
14 _____
15 _____
16 _____
17 _____
18 _____
19 _____
20 _____
21 _____
22 _____
23 _____
24 _____
25 _____
26 _____
27 _____
28 _____
29 _____
30 _____
31 _____

OCTOBER MEMORIES

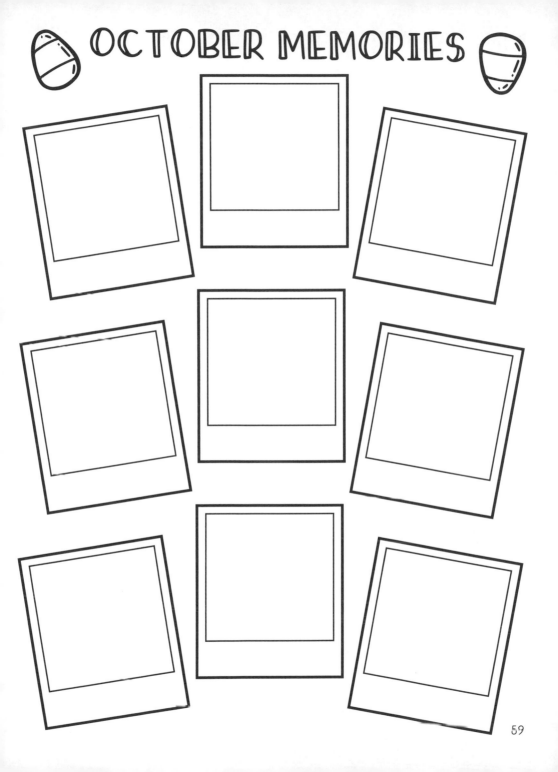

NOVEMBER MOOD TRACKER

FILL OUT THE KEY, AND COLOR THE DAILY ICON TO REPRESENT YOUR MOOD!

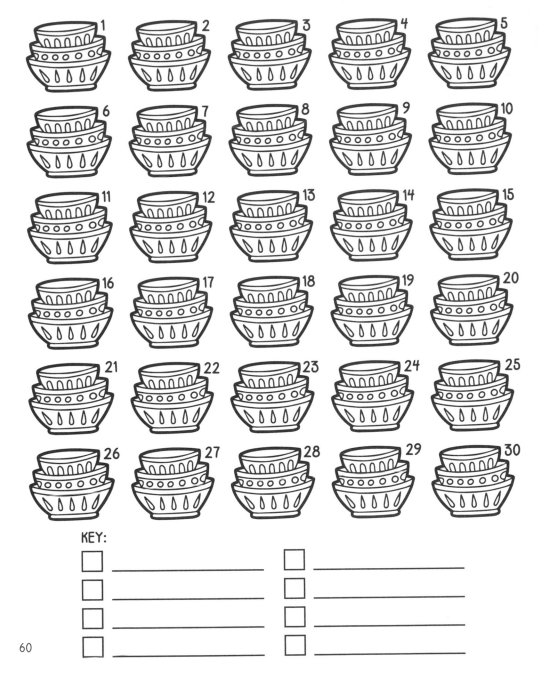

KEY:

☐ _____   ☐ _____

☐ _____   ☐ _____

☐ _____   ☐ _____

☐ _____   ☐ _____

NOVEMBER GRATITUDE

RECORD 1 LINE OF GRATITUDE EACH DAY!

1 _____
2 _____
3 _____
4 _____
5 _____
6 _____
7 _____
8 _____
9 _____
10 _____
11 _____
12 _____
13 _____
14 _____
15 _____
16 _____
17 _____
18 _____
19 _____
20 _____
21 _____
22 _____
23 _____
24 _____
25 _____
26 _____
27 _____
28 _____
29 _____
30 _____

NOVEMBER MEMORIES

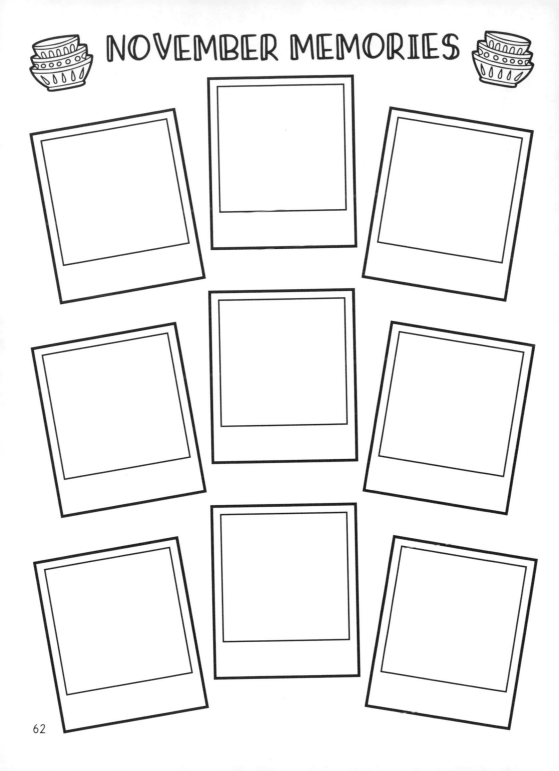

DECEMBER MOOD TRACKER

FILL OUT THE KEY, AND COLOR THE DAILY ICON TO REPRESENT YOUR MOOD!

KEY:

☐ _____ ☐ _____
☐ _____ ☐ _____
☐ _____ ☐ _____
☐ _____ ☐ _____

63

DECEMBER GRATITUDE

RECORD 1 LINE OF GRATITUDE EACH DAY!

1 _____
2 _____
3 _____
4 _____
5 _____
6 _____
7 _____
8 _____
9 _____
10 _____
11 _____
12 _____
13 _____
14 _____
15 _____
16 _____
17 _____
18 _____
19 _____
20 _____
21 _____
22 _____
23 _____
24 _____
25 _____
26 _____
27 _____
28 _____
29 _____
30 _____
31 _____

❄ DECEMBER MEMORIES ❄

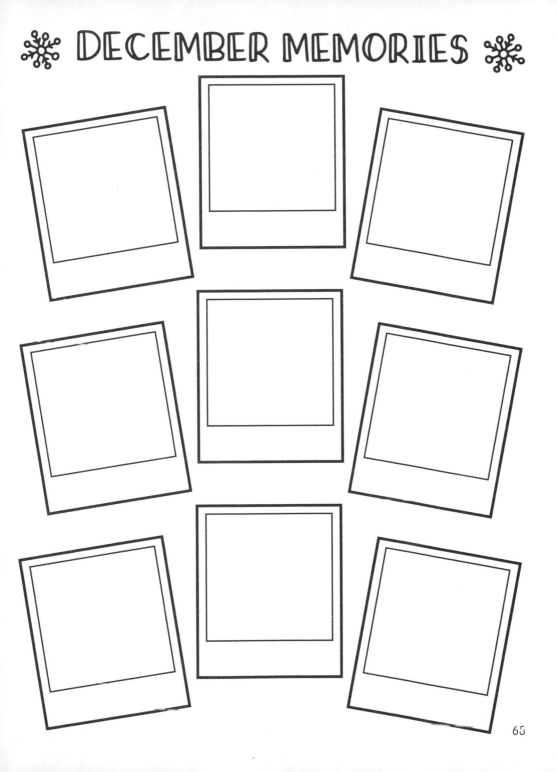

WEEKLY HABIT TRACKERS

TRACK YOUR HABITS ON A WEEKLY BASIS TO SET SMALL, REALISTIC GOALS!

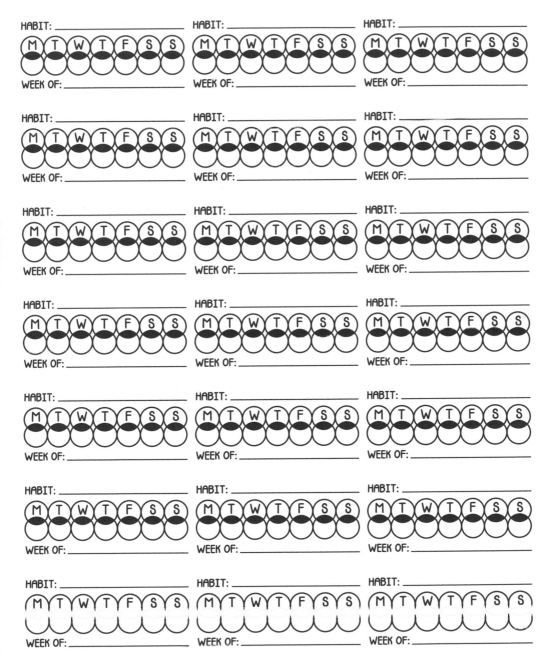

HABIT: _____

(M)(T)(W)(T)(F)(S)(S)

WEEK OF: _____

HABIT: _____

(M)(T)(W)(T)(F)(S)(S)

WEEK OF: _____

HABIT: _____

(M)(T)(W)(T)(F)(S)(S)

WEEK OF: _____

HABIT: _____

(M)(T)(W)(T)(F)(S)(S)

WEEK OF: _____

HABIT: _____

(M)(T)(W)(T)(F)(S)(S)

WEEK OF: _____

HABIT: _____

(M)(T)(W)(T)(F)(S)(S)

WEEK OF: _____

HABIT: _____

(M)(T)(W)(T)(F)(S)(S)

WEEK OF: _____

HABIT: _____

(M)(T)(W)(T)(F)(S)(S)

WEEK OF: _____

HABIT: _____

(M)(T)(W)(T)(F)(S)(S)

WEEK OF: _____

HABIT: _____

(M)(T)(W)(T)(F)(S)(S)

WEEK OF: _____

HABIT: _____

(M)(T)(W)(T)(F)(S)(S)

WEEK OF: _____

HABIT: _____

(M)(T)(W)(T)(F)(S)(S)

WEEK OF: _____

HABIT: _____

(M)(T)(W)(T)(F)(S)(S)

WEEK OF: _____

HABIT: _____

(M)(T)(W)(T)(F)(S)(S)

WEEK OF: _____

HABIT: _____

(M)(T)(W)(T)(F)(S)(S)

WEEK OF: _____

HABIT: _____

(M)(T)(W)(T)(F)(S)(S)

WEEK OF: _____

HABIT: _____

(M)(T)(W)(T)(F)(S)(S)

WEEK OF: _____

HABIT: _____

(M)(T)(W)(T)(F)(S)(S)

WEEK OF: _____

HABIT: _____

(M)(T)(W)(T)(F)(S)(S)

WEEK OF: _____

HABIT: _____

(M)(T)(W)(T)(F)(S)(S)

WEEK OF: _____

HABIT: _____

(M)(T)(W)(T)(F)(S)(S)

WEEK OF: _____

HABIT: _____
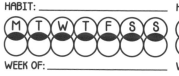
WEEK OF: _____

HABIT: _____
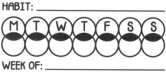
WEEK OF: _____

HABIT: _____
WEEK OF: _____

HABIT: _____
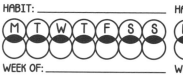
WEEK OF: _____

HABIT: _____
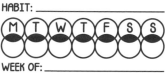
WEEK OF: _____

HABIT: _____
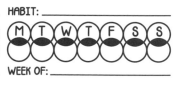
WEEK OF: _____

HABIT: _____
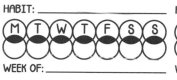
WEEK OF: _____

HABIT: _____
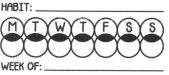
WEEK OF: _____

HABIT: _____
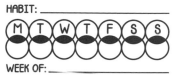
WEEK OF: _____

HABIT: _____
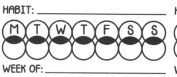
WEEK OF: _____

HABIT: _____
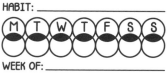
WEEK OF: _____

HABIT: _____
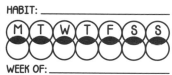
WEEK OF: _____

HABIT: _____
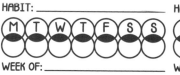
WEEK OF: _____

HABIT: _____

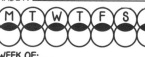
WEEK OF: _____

HABIT: _____
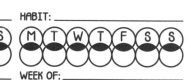
WEEK OF: _____

HABIT: _____
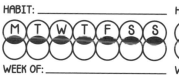
WEEK OF: _____

HABIT: _____
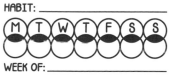
WEEK OF: _____

HABIT: _____
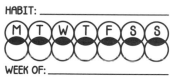
WEEK OF: _____

HABIT: _____
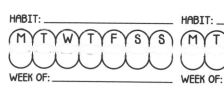
WEEK OF: _____

HABIT: _____
WEEK OF: _____

HABIT: _____
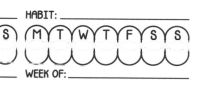
WEEK OF: _____

IMPORTANT

JANUARY

_____ _____
_____ _____
_____ _____
_____ _____
_____ _____
_____ _____
_____ _____
_____ _____
_____ _____
_____ _____
_____ _____
_____ _____

FEBRUARY

_____ _____
_____ _____
_____ _____
_____ _____
_____ _____
_____ _____
_____ _____
_____ _____
_____ _____
_____ _____
_____ _____
_____ _____

MARCH

_____ _____
_____ _____
_____ _____
_____ _____
_____ _____
_____ _____
_____ _____
_____ _____
_____ _____
_____ _____
_____ _____
_____ _____

JULY

_____ _____
_____ _____
_____ _____
_____ _____
_____ _____
_____ _____
_____ _____
_____ _____
_____ _____
_____ _____
_____ _____
_____ _____

AUGUST

_____ _____
_____ _____
_____ _____
_____ _____
_____ _____
_____ _____
_____ _____
_____ _____
_____ _____
_____ _____
_____ _____
_____ _____

SEPTEMBER

_____ _____
_____ _____
_____ _____
_____ _____
_____ _____
_____ _____
_____ _____
_____ _____
_____ _____
_____ _____
_____ _____
_____ _____

DATES

APRIL

_____ _____
_____ _____
_____ _____
_____ _____
_____ _____
_____ _____
_____ _____
_____ _____
_____ _____
_____ _____
_____ _____

MAY

_____ _____
_____ _____
_____ _____
_____ _____
_____ _____
_____ _____
_____ _____
_____ _____
_____ _____
_____ _____
_____ _____

JUNE

_____ _____
_____ _____
_____ _____
_____ _____
_____ _____
_____ _____
_____ _____
_____ _____
_____ _____
_____ _____
_____ _____

OCTOBER

_____ _____
_____ _____
_____ _____
_____ _____
_____ _____
_____ _____
_____ _____
_____ _____
_____ _____
_____ _____
_____ _____

NOVEMBER

_____ _____
_____ _____
_____ _____
_____ _____
_____ _____
_____ _____
_____ _____
_____ _____
_____ _____
_____ _____
_____ _____

DECEMBER

_____ _____
_____ _____
_____ _____
_____ _____
_____ _____
_____ _____
_____ _____
_____ _____
_____ _____
_____ _____
_____ _____

BIRTHDAY

JANUARY

FEBRUARY

MARCH

_____   _____
_____   _____
_____   _____
_____   _____
_____   _____

JULY

AUGUST

SEPTEMBER

_____   _____
_____   _____
_____   _____
_____   _____

TRACKER

APRIL

MAY

JUNE

---- ---- ----
---- ---- ----
---- ---- ----
---- ---- ----
---- ---- ----

OCTOBER

NOVEMBER

DECEMBER

---- ---- ----
---- ---- ----
---- ---- ----
---- ---- ----
---- ---- ----

BUCKET LIST

- [ ] _____
- [ ] _____
- [ ] _____
- [ ] _____
- [ ] _____
- [ ] _____
- [ ] _____
- [ ] _____
- [ ] _____
- [ ] _____
- [ ] _____
- [ ] _____
- [ ] _____
- [ ] _____
- [ ] _____
- [ ] _____
- [ ] _____
- [ ] _____
- [ ] _____
- [ ] _____
- [ ] _____
- [ ] _____

RESOLUTIONS

WHO NEEDS A NEW YEAR TO MAKE RESOLUTIONS? START TODAY!

DATE: _____
RESOLUTION: _____
_____
_____
_____
_____

DATE: _____
RESOLUTION: _____
_____
_____
_____
_____

DATE: _____
RESOLUTION: _____
_____
_____
_____
_____

DATE: _____
RESOLUTION: _____
_____
_____
_____
_____

DATE: _____
RESOLUTION: _____
_____
_____
_____
_____

DATE: _____
RESOLUTION: _____
_____
_____
_____
_____

DATE: _____
RESOLUTION: _____
_____
_____
_____
_____

DATE: _____
RESOLUTION: _____
_____
_____
_____
_____

DATE: _____
RESOLUTION: _____
_____
_____
_____
_____

DATE: _____
RESOLUTION: _____
_____
_____
_____
_____

DATE: _____
RESOLUTION: _____
_____
_____
_____
_____

DATE: _____
RESOLUTION: _____
_____
_____
_____
_____

30-DAY CHALLENGES

HAVE A GOAL? THINK YOU CAN REACH IT IN 30 DAYS?
TRY OUT THESE TRACKERS!

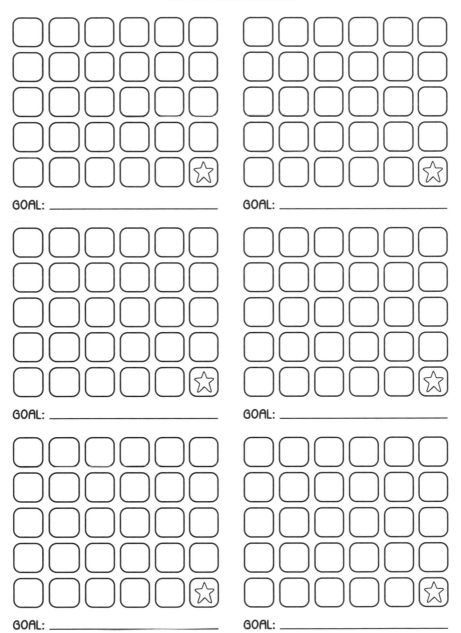

GOAL: _____

GOAL: _____

GOAL: _____

GOAL: _____

GOAL: _____

GOAL: _____

MEDICAL APPOINTMENT TRACKER

PHYSICIAN: _____
ADDRESS: _____
PHONE NUMBER: _____
REASON: _____
DIAGNOSIS: _____
MEDICATION: _____
NOTES: _____
_____
_____

PHYSICIAN: _____
ADDRESS: _____
PHONE NUMBER: _____
REASON: _____
DIAGNOSIS: _____
MEDICATION: _____
NOTES: _____
_____
_____

PHYSICIAN: _____
ADDRESS: _____
PHONE NUMBER: _____
REASON: _____
DIAGNOSIS: _____
MEDICATION: _____
NOTES: _____
_____
_____

PHYSICIAN: _____
ADDRESS: _____
PHONE NUMBER: _____
REASON: _____
DIAGNOSIS: _____
MEDICATION: _____
NOTES: _____
_____
_____

PHYSICIAN: _____
ADDRESS: _____
PHONE NUMBER: _____
REASON: _____
DIAGNOSIS: _____
MEDICATION: _____
NOTES: _____
_____
_____

PHYSICIAN: _____
ADDRESS: _____
PHONE NUMBER: _____
REASON: _____
DIAGNOSIS: _____
MEDICATION: _____
NOTES: _____
_____
_____

PHYSICIAN: _____
ADDRESS: _____
PHONE NUMBER: _____
REASON: _____
DIAGNOSIS: _____
MEDICATION: _____
NOTES: _____
_____
_____

PHYSICIAN: _____
ADDRESS: _____
PHONE NUMBER: _____
REASON: _____
DIAGNOSIS: _____
MEDICATION: _____
NOTES: _____
_____
_____

YEARLY MEDICATION TRACKER

DID YOU TAKE YOUR MEDICATION/VITAMINS TODAY?

	J	F	M	A	M	J	J	A	S	O	N	D
1	○	○	○	○	○	○	○	○	○	○	○	○
2	○	○	○	○	○	○	○	○	○	○	○	○
3	○	○	○	○	○	○	○	○	○	○	○	○
4	○	○	○	○	○	○	○	○	○	○	○	○
5	○	○	○	○	○	○	○	○	○	○	○	○
6	○	○	○	○	○	○	○	○	○	○	○	○
7	○	○	○	○	○	○	○	○	○	○	○	○
8	○	○	○	○	○	○	○	○	○	○	○	○
9	○	○	○	○	○	○	○	○	○	○	○	○
10	○	○	○	○	○	○	○	○	○	○	○	○
11	○	○	○	○	○	○	○	○	○	○	○	○
12	○	○	○	○	○	○	○	○	○	○	○	○
13	○	○	○	○	○	○	○	○	○	○	○	○
14	○	○	○	○	○	○	○	○	○	○	○	○
15	○	○	○	○	○	○	○	○	○	○	○	○
16	○	○	○	○	○	○	○	○	○	○	○	○
17	○	○	○	○	○	○	○	○	○	○	○	○
18	○	○	○	○	○	○	○	○	○	○	○	○
19	○	○	○	○	○	○	○	○	○	○	○	○
20	○	○	○	○	○	○	○	○	○	○	○	○
21	○	○	○	○	○	○	○	○	○	○	○	○
22	○	○	○	○	○	○	○	○	○	○	○	○
23	○	○	○	○	○	○	○	○	○	○	○	○
24	○	○	○	○	○	○	○	○	○	○	○	○
25	○	○	○	○	○	○	○	○	○	○	○	○
26	○	○	○	○	○	○	○	○	○	○	○	○
27	○	○	○	○	○	○	○	○	○	○	○	○
28	○	○	○	○	○	○	○	○	○	○	○	○
29	○	⦙	○	○	○	○	○	○	○	○	○	○
30	○		○	○	○	○	○	○	○	○	○	○
31	○		○		○		○	○		○		○

YEARLY SYMPTOM TRACKER

IF YOU FEEL OFF, FILL IN THE CORRESPONDING DAILY CIRCLE.

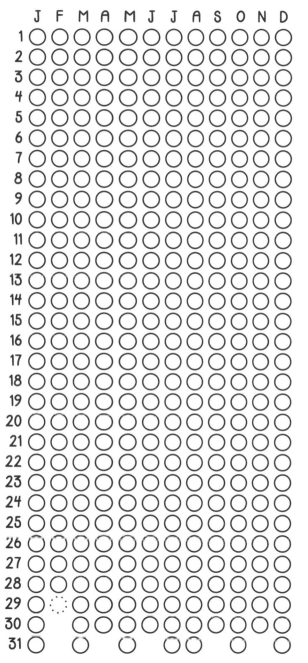

MEDICATION INFORMATION

MEDICATION: _____
DOSE: _____
FREQUENCY: _____
SIDE EFFECTS: _____
_____

MEDICATION: _____
DOSE: _____
FREQUENCY: _____
SIDE EFFECTS: _____
_____

MEDICATION: _____
DOSE: _____
FREQUENCY: _____
SIDE EFFECTS: _____
_____

MEDICATION: _____
DOSE: _____
FREQUENCY: _____
SIDE EFFECTS: _____
_____

MEDICATION: _____
DOSE: _____
FREQUENCY: _____
SIDE EFFECTS: _____
_____

MEDICATION: _____
DOSE: _____
FREQUENCY: _____
SIDE EFFECTS: _____
_____

MEDICATION: _____
DOSE: _____
FREQUENCY: _____
SIDE EFFECTS: _____
_____

MEDICATION: _____
DOSE: _____
FREQUENCY: _____
SIDE EFFECTS: _____
_____

MEDICATION: _____
DOSE: _____
FREQUENCY: _____
SIDE EFFECTS: _____
_____

MEDICATION: _____
DOSE: _____
FREQUENCY: _____
SIDE EFFECTS: _____
_____

MEDICATION: _____
DOSE: _____
FREQUENCY: _____
SIDE EFFECTS: _____
_____

MEDICATION: _____
DOSE: _____
FREQUENCY: _____
SIDE EFFECTS: _____
_____

MEDICATION: _____
DOSE: _____
FREQUENCY: _____
SIDE EFFECTS: _____
_____

MEDICATION: _____
DOSE: _____
FREQUENCY: _____
SIDE EFFECTS: _____
_____

MEDICATION: _____
DOSE: _____
FREQUENCY: _____
SIDE EFFECTS: _____
_____

MEDICATION: _____
DOSE: _____
FREQUENCY: _____
SIDE EFFECTS: _____
_____

MEDICATION: _____
DOSE: _____
FREQUENCY: _____
SIDE EFFECTS: _____
_____

MEDICATION: _____
DOSE: _____
FREQUENCY: _____
SIDE EFFECTS: _____
_____

MEDICATION: _____
DOSE: _____
FREQUENCY: _____
SIDE EFFECTS: _____
_____

MEDICATION: _____
DOSE: _____
FREQUENCY: _____
SIDE EFFECTS: _____
_____

MEDICATION: _____
DOSE: _____
FREQUENCY: _____
SIDE EFFECTS: _____
_____

MEDICATION: _____
DOSE: _____
FREQUENCY: _____
SIDE EFFECTS: _____
_____

MEDICATION: _____
DOSE: _____
FREQUENCY: _____
SIDE EFFECTS: _____
_____

MEDICATION: _____
DOSE: _____
FREQUENCY: _____
SIDE EFFECTS: _____
_____

MEDICATION: _____
DOSE: _____
FREQUENCY: _____
SIDE EFFECTS: _____
_____

MEDICATION: _____
DOSE: _____
FREQUENCY: _____
SIDE EFFECTS: _____
_____

MEDICATION: _____
DOSE: _____
FREQUENCY: _____
SIDE EFFECTS: _____
_____

MEDICATION: _____
DOSE: _____
FREQUENCY: _____
SIDE EFFECTS: _____
_____

DENTAL TRACKER

DATE: _____
DENTIST: _____
REASON FOR APPOINTMENT: _____

NOTES: _____
_____
_____

DATE: _____
DENTIST: _____
REASON FOR APPOINTMENT: _____

NOTES: _____
_____
_____

DATE: _____
DENTIST: _____
REASON FOR APPOINTMENT: _____

NOTES: _____
_____
_____

DATE: _____
DENTIST: _____
REASON FOR APPOINTMENT: _____

NOTES: _____
_____
_____

DATE: _____
DENTIST: _____
REASON FOR APPOINTMENT: _____

NOTES: _____
_____
_____

DATE: _____
DENTIST: _____
REASON FOR APPOINTMENT: _____

NOTES: _____
_____
_____

DATE: _____
DENTIST: _____
REASON FOR APPOINTMENT: _____

NOTES: _____
_____
_____

DATE: _____
DENTIST: _____
REASON FOR APPOINTMENT: _____

NOTES: _____
_____
_____

PAIN TRACKER
IN PAIN? FEELING OFF? TRACK IT!

DATE: _____
PAIN DESCRIPTION: _____
_____
DURATION: _____
POSSIBLE CAUSE: _____
_____
INTENSITY:
① ② ③ ④ ⑤ ⑥ ⑦ ⑧ ⑨ ⑩
NOTES: _____
_____
_____

DATE: _____
PAIN DESCRIPTION: _____
_____
DURATION: _____
POSSIBLE CAUSE: _____
_____
INTENSITY:
① ② ③ ④ ⑤ ⑥ ⑦ ⑧ ⑨ ⑩
NOTES: _____
_____
_____

DATE: _____
PAIN DESCRIPTION: _____
_____
DURATION: _____
POSSIBLE CAUSE: _____
_____
INTENSITY:
① ② ③ ④ ⑤ ⑥ ⑦ ⑧ ⑨ ⑩
NOTES: _____
_____
_____

DATE: _____
PAIN DESCRIPTION: _____
_____
DURATION: _____
POSSIBLE CAUSE: _____
_____
INTENSITY:
① ② ③ ④ ⑤ ⑥ ⑦ ⑧ ⑨ ⑩
NOTES: _____
_____
_____

DATE: _____
PAIN DESCRIPTION: _____
_____
DURATION: _____
POSSIBLE CAUSE: _____
_____
INTENSITY:
① ② ③ ④ ⑤ ⑥ ⑦ ⑧ ⑨ ⑩
NOTES: _____
_____
_____

DATE: _____
PAIN DESCRIPTION: _____
_____
DURATION: _____
POSSIBLE CAUSE: _____
_____
INTENSITY:
① ② ③ ④ ⑤ ⑥ ⑦ ⑧ ⑨ ⑩
NOTES: _____
_____
_____

SLEEP TRACKER

SAMPLE THE QUALITY OF YOUR ZZZS.

DATE: _____
LENGTH: 0 1 2 3 4 5 6 7 8 9 10 11 12
QUALITY: ☆ ☆ ☆ ☆ ☆
NOTES: _____
_____
_____

DATE: _____
LENGTH: 0 1 2 3 4 5 6 7 8 9 10 11 12
QUALITY: ☆ ☆ ☆ ☆ ☆
NOTES: _____
_____
_____

DATE: _____
LENGTH: 0 1 2 3 4 5 6 7 8 9 10 11 12
QUALITY: ☆ ☆ ☆ ☆ ☆
NOTES: _____
_____
_____

DATE: _____
LENGTH: 0 1 2 3 4 5 6 7 8 9 10 11 12
QUALITY: ☆ ☆ ☆ ☆ ☆
NOTES: _____
_____
_____

DATE: _____
LENGTH: 0 1 2 3 4 5 6 7 8 9 10 11 12
QUALITY: ☆ ☆ ☆ ☆ ☆
NOTES: _____
_____
_____

DATE: _____
LENGTH: 0 1 2 3 4 5 6 7 8 9 10 11 12
QUALITY: ☆ ☆ ☆ ☆ ☆
NOTES: _____
_____
_____

DATE: _____
LENGTH: 0 1 2 3 4 5 6 7 8 9 10 11 12
QUALITY: ☆ ☆ ☆ ☆ ☆
NOTES: _____
_____
_____

DATE: _____
LENGTH: 0 1 2 3 4 5 6 7 8 9 10 11 12
QUALITY: ☆ ☆ ☆ ☆ ☆
NOTES: _____
_____
_____

DATE: _____
LENGTH: 0 1 2 3 4 5 6 7 8 9 10 11 12
QUALITY: ☆ ☆ ☆ ☆ ☆
NOTES: _____
_____
_____

DATE: _____
LENGTH: 0 1 2 3 4 5 6 7 8 9 10 11 12
QUALITY: ☆ ☆ ☆ ☆ ☆
NOTES: _____
_____
_____

DATE: _____
LENGTH: 0 1 2 3 4 5 6 7 8 9 10 11 12
QUALITY: ☆ ☆ ☆ ☆ ☆
NOTES: _____
_____
_____

DATE: _____
LENGTH: 0 1 2 3 4 5 6 7 8 9 10 11 12
QUALITY: ☆ ☆ ☆ ☆ ☆
NOTES: _____
_____
_____

DATE: _____
LENGTH: 0 1 2 3 4 5 6 7 8 9 10 11 12
QUALITY: ☆ ☆ ☆ ☆ ☆
NOTES: _____
_____
_____

DATE: _____
LENGTH: 0 1 2 3 4 5 6 7 8 9 10 11 12
QUALITY: ☆ ☆ ☆ ☆ ☆
NOTES: _____
_____
_____

DATE: _____
LENGTH: 0 1 2 3 4 5 6 7 8 9 10 11 12
QUALITY: ☆ ☆ ☆ ☆ ☆
NOTES: _____
_____
_____

DATE: _____
LENGTH: 0 1 2 3 4 5 6 7 8 9 10 11 12
QUALITY: ☆ ☆ ☆ ☆ ☆
NOTES: _____
_____
_____

DATE: _____
LENGTH: 0 1 2 3 4 5 6 7 8 9 10 11 12
QUALITY: ☆ ☆ ☆ ☆ ☆
NOTES: _____
_____
_____

DATE: _____
LENGTH: 0 1 2 3 4 5 6 7 8 9 10 11 12
QUALITY: ☆ ☆ ☆ ☆ ☆
NOTES: _____
_____
_____

WEEKLY WATER TRACKERS

AS THEY SAY, IT'S 8 GLASSES A DAY! EACH WATER BOTTLE HAS 8 SECTIONS TO FILL IN.
EACH DAY, FILL IN A SECTION OF THE WATER BOTTLE FOR EVERY GLASS OF WATER YOU DRINK!

WEEK OF:_____

WEEK OF:_____

WEEK OF:_____

WEEK OF:_____

WEEK OF:_____

WEEK OF:_____

WEEK OF:_____

WEEK OF:_____

WEEK OF:_____

WEEK OF:_____

WEEK OF:_____

WEEK OF:_____

WEEK OF:_____

WEEK OF:_____

WEEK OF:_____

WEEK OF:_____

WEEK OF:_____

WEEK OF:_____

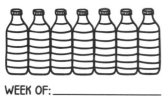

WEEK OF:_____

WEEK OF:_____

WEEK OF:_____

WEEK OF:_____

WEEK OF:_____

WEEK OF:_____

WEEK OF:_____

WEEK OF:_____

WEEK OF:_____

WEEK OF:_____

WEEK OF:_____

WEEK OF:_____

WEEK OF:_____

WEEK OF:_____

WEIGHT TRACKER

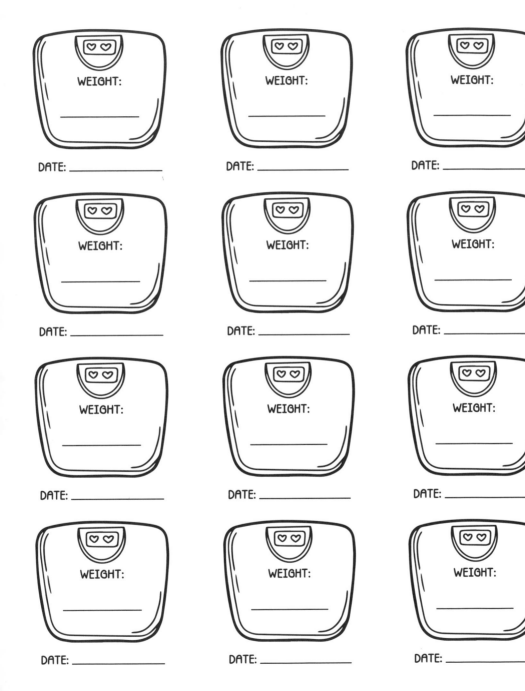

WEIGHT:

_____

DATE: _____

WEIGHT:

_____

DATE: _____

WEIGHT:

_____

DATE: _____

WEIGHT:

_____

DATE: _____

WEIGHT:

_____

DATE: _____

WEIGHT:

_____

DATE: _____

WEIGHT:

_____

DATE: _____

WEIGHT:

_____

DATE: _____

WEIGHT:

_____

DATE: _____

WEIGHT:

_____

DATE: _____

WEIGHT:

_____

DATE: _____

WEIGHT:

_____

DATE: _____

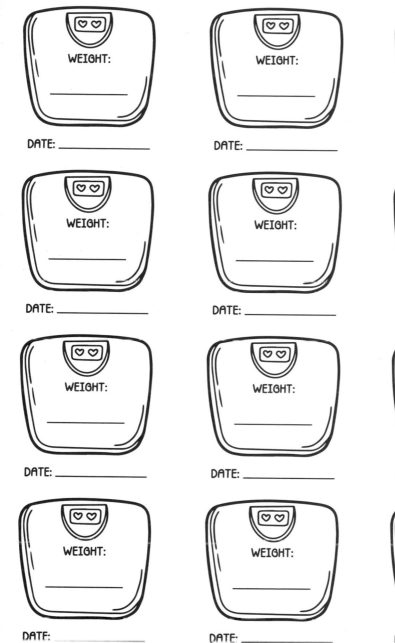

WEIGHT:
_____

DATE: _____

WEIGHT:
_____

DATE: _____

WEIGHT:
_____

DATE: _____

WEIGHT:
_____

DATE: _____

WEIGHT:
_____

DATE: _____

WEIGHT:
_____

DATE: _____

WEIGHT:
_____

DATE: _____

WEIGHT:
_____

DATE: _____

WEIGHT:
_____

DATE: _____

WEIGHT:
_____

DATE: _____

WEIGHT:
_____

DATE: _____

WEIGHT:
_____

DATE: _____

BODY MEASUREMENTS

GOING THROUGH A BIG CHANGE?
KEEP TRACK!

DATE: _____

CHEST: _____
LEFT ARM: _____
RIGHT ARM: _____
WAIST: _____
HIPS: _____
LEFT THIGH: _____
RIGHT THIGH: _____
LEFT CALF: _____
RIGHT CALF: _____

DATE: _____

CHEST: _____
LEFT ARM: _____
RIGHT ARM: _____
WAIST: _____
HIPS: _____
LEFT THIGH: _____
RIGHT THIGH: _____
LEFT CALF: _____
RIGHT CALF: _____

DATE: _____

CHEST: _____
LEFT ARM: _____
RIGHT ARM: _____
WAIST: _____
HIPS: _____
LEFT THIGH: _____
RIGHT THIGH: _____
LEFT CALF: _____
RIGHT CALF: _____

DATE: _____

CHEST: _____
LEFT ARM: _____
RIGHT ARM: _____
WAIST: _____
HIPS: _____
LEFT THIGH: _____
RIGHT THIGH: _____
LEFT CALF: _____
RIGHT CALF: _____

DATE: _____

CHEST: _____
LEFT ARM: _____
RIGHT ARM: _____
WAIST: _____
HIPS: _____
LEFT THIGH: _____
RIGHT THIGH: _____
LEFT CALF: _____
RIGHT CALF: _____

DATE: _____

CHEST: _____
LEFT ARM: _____
RIGHT ARM: _____
WAIST: _____
HIPS: _____
LEFT THIGH: _____
RIGHT THIGH: _____
LEFT CALF: _____
RIGHT CALF: _____

DATE: _____

CHEST: _____
LEFT ARM: _____
RIGHT ARM: _____
WAIST: _____
HIPS: _____
LEFT THIGH: _____
RIGHT THIGH: _____
LEFT CALF: _____
RIGHT CALF: _____

DATE: _____

CHEST: _____
LEFT ARM: _____
RIGHT ARM: _____
WAIST: _____
HIPS: _____
LEFT THIGH: _____
RIGHT THIGH: _____
LEFT CALF: _____
RIGHT CALF: _____

30-DAY STEP TRACKING

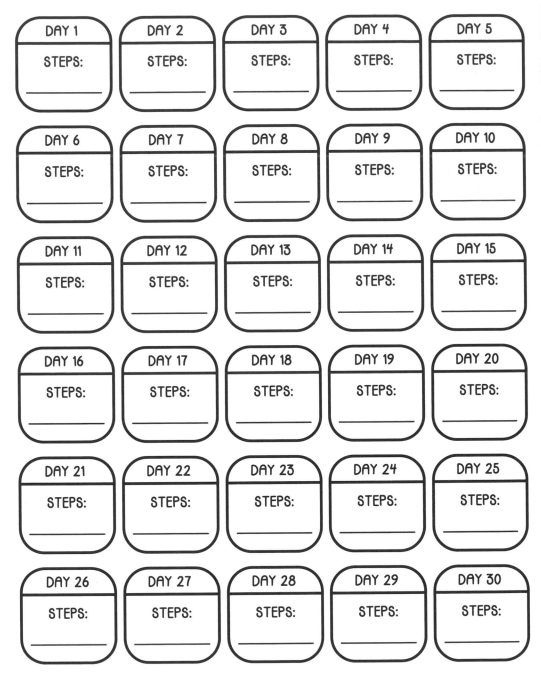

DAY 1	DAY 2	DAY 3	DAY 4	DAY 5
STEPS:	STEPS:	STEPS:	STEPS:	STEPS:
DAY 6	DAY 7	DAY 8	DAY 9	DAY 10
STEPS:	STEPS:	STEPS:	STEPS:	STEPS:
DAY 11	DAY 12	DAY 13	DAY 14	DAY 15
STEPS:	STEPS:	STEPS:	STEPS:	STEPS:
DAY 16	DAY 17	DAY 18	DAY 19	DAY 20
STEPS:	STEPS:	STEPS:	STEPS:	STEPS:
DAY 21	DAY 22	DAY 23	DAY 24	DAY 25
STEPS:	STEPS:	STEPS:	STEPS:	STEPS:
DAY 26	DAY 27	DAY 28	DAY 29	DAY 30
STEPS:	STEPS:	STEPS:	STEPS:	STEPS:

PERIOD TRACKER

FILL OUT THE KEY, AND TRACK YOUR PERIOD THROUGHOUT THE YEAR.

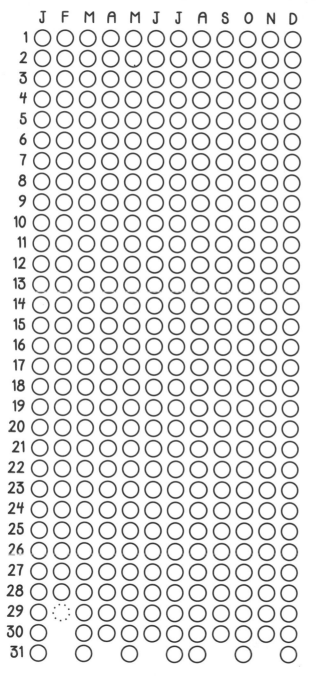

KEY:
- ○ HEAVY
- ○ NORMAL
- ○ LIGHT
- ○ SPOTTING
- ○ CRAMPS
- ○ MOODY

CLEANING TRACKER

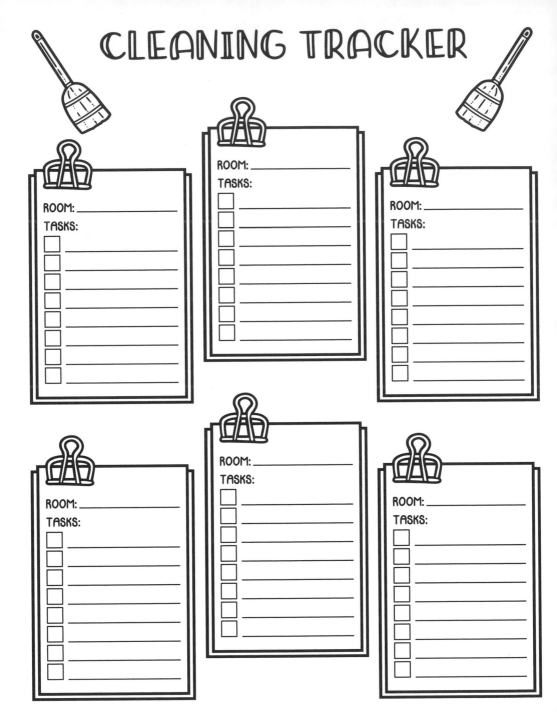

ROOM: _____

TASKS:

- ☐ _____
- ☐ _____
- ☐ _____
- ☐ _____
- ☐ _____
- ☐ _____
- ☐ _____
- ☐ _____

ROOM: _____

TASKS:

- ☐ _____
- ☐ _____
- ☐ _____
- ☐ _____
- ☐ _____
- ☐ _____
- ☐ _____
- ☐ _____

ROOM: _____

TASKS:

- ☐ _____
- ☐ _____
- ☐ _____
- ☐ _____
- ☐ _____
- ☐ _____
- ☐ _____
- ☐ _____

ROOM: _____

TASKS:

- ☐ _____
- ☐ _____
- ☐ _____
- ☐ _____
- ☐ _____
- ☐ _____
- ☐ _____
- ☐ _____

ROOM: _____

TASKS:

- ☐ _____
- ☐ _____
- ☐ _____
- ☐ _____
- ☐ _____
- ☐ _____
- ☐ _____
- ☐ _____

ROOM: _____

TASKS:

- ☐ _____
- ☐ _____
- ☐ _____
- ☐ _____
- ☐ _____
- ☐ _____
- ☐ _____
- ☐ _____

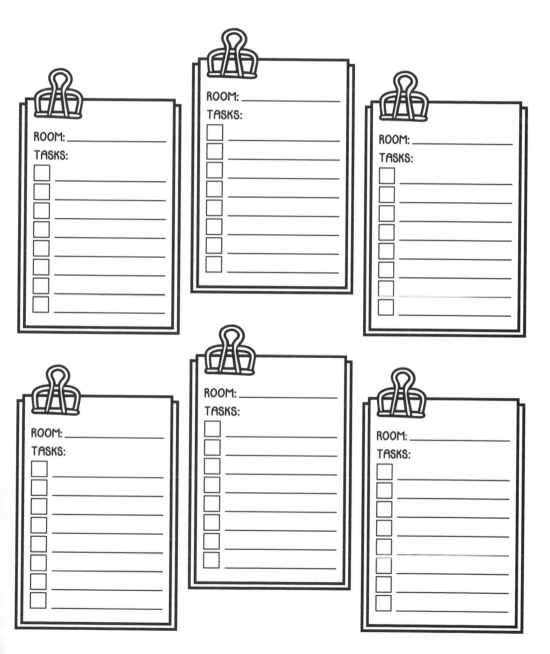

ROOM: _____

TASKS:

☐ _____
☐ _____
☐ _____
☐ _____
☐ _____
☐ _____
☐ _____
☐ _____

ROOM: _____

TASKS:

☐ _____
☐ _____
☐ _____
☐ _____
☐ _____
☐ _____
☐ _____
☐ _____

ROOM: _____

TASKS:

☐ _____
☐ _____
☐ _____
☐ _____
☐ _____
☐ _____
☐ _____
☐ _____

ROOM: _____

TASKS:

☐ _____
☐ _____
☐ _____
☐ _____
☐ _____
☐ _____
☐ _____
☐ _____

ROOM: _____

TASKS:

☐ _____
☐ _____
☐ _____
☐ _____
☐ _____
☐ _____
☐ _____
☐ _____

ROOM: _____

TASKS:

☐ _____
☐ _____
☐ _____
☐ _____
☐ _____
☐ _____
☐ _____
☐ _____

CHORE CHART

SPLIT UP THOSE CHORES AND GET THINGS DONE!

ASSIGNED TO:	CHORE:	COMPLETED ON:

HOME PROJECT TRACKER

IS YOUR HOME IN NEED OF SOME IMPROVEMENT?
TRACK PROJECTS AND CHECK THEM OFF WHEN THEY'RE COMPLETED!

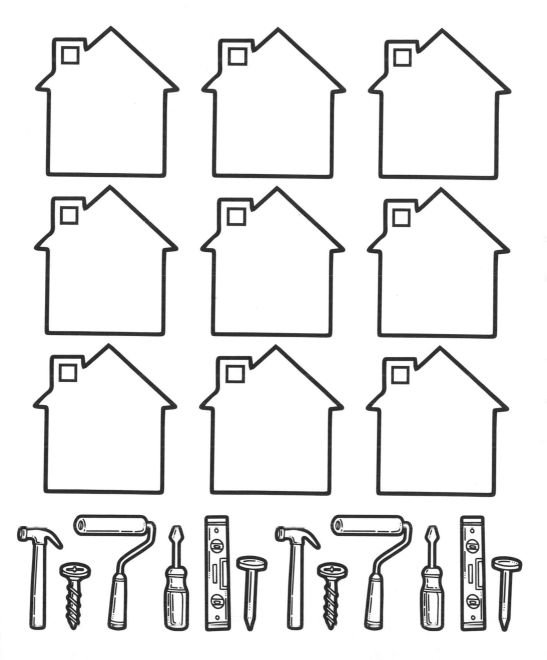

LAWN CARE TRACKER

SERVICE/JOB/PROJECT: **DATE/TIME COMPLETED:**

- ☐ _____   _____
- ☐ _____   _____
- ☐ _____   _____
- ☐ _____   _____
- ☐ _____   _____
- ☐ _____   _____
- ☐ _____   _____
- ☐ _____   _____
- ☐ _____   _____
- ☐ _____   _____
- ☐ _____   _____
- ☐ _____   _____
- ☐ _____   _____
- ☐ _____   _____
- ☐ _____   _____
- ☐ _____   _____
- ☐ _____   _____
- ☐ _____   _____
- ☐ _____   _____
- ☐ _____   _____

HOUSEPLANT CARE TRACKER

CHECK IN WITH YOUR GREEN FRIENDS! EXPAND IN A PERSONAL NOTEBOOK AS NEEDED.

PLANT: _____

CARE NOTES: _____

_____

_____

_____

LAST WATERED:

_____ _____

_____ _____

_____ _____

PLANT: _____

CARE NOTES: _____

_____

_____

_____

LAST WATERED:

_____ _____

_____ _____

_____ _____

PLANT: _____

CARE NOTES: _____

_____

_____

_____

LAST WATERED:

_____ _____

_____ _____

_____ _____

PLANT: _____

CARE NOTES: _____

_____

_____

_____

LAST WATERED:

_____ _____

_____ _____

_____ _____

PLANT: _____

CARE NOTES: _____

_____

_____

_____

LAST WATERED:

_____ _____

_____ _____

_____ _____

PLANT: _____

CARE NOTES: _____

_____

_____

_____

LAST WATERED:

_____ _____

_____ _____

_____ _____

MOVING TASK TRACKER

TIME TO MOVE? KEEP TRACK OF YOUR TASK LIST!

TASK: DATE/TIME COMPLETED:

☐ _____   _____
☐ _____   _____
☐ _____   _____
☐ _____   _____
☐ _____   _____
☐ _____   _____
☐ _____   _____
☐ _____   _____
☐ _____   _____
☐ _____   _____
☐ _____   _____
☐ _____   _____
☐ _____   _____
☐ _____   _____
☐ _____   _____
☐ _____   _____
☐ _____   _____
☐ _____   _____
☐ _____   _____
☐ _____   _____

TASK: DATE/TIME COMPLETED:

☐ _____   _____
☐ _____   _____
☐ _____   _____
☐ _____   _____
☐ _____   _____
☐ _____   _____
☐ _____   _____
☐ _____   _____
☐ _____   _____
☐ _____   _____
☐ _____   _____
☐ _____   _____
☐ _____   _____
☐ _____   _____
☐ _____   _____
☐ _____   _____
☐ _____   _____
☐ _____   _____
☐ _____   _____
☐ _____   _____

PACKING LIST

MOVING SOON?
KEEP TRACK OF PACKING EACH ROOM!

ROOM: _____
○ ○ ○

ROOM: _____
○ ○ ○ ○ ○

ROOM: _____
○ ○ ○ ○ ○ ○ ○

ROOM: _____
○ ○ ○ ○ ○ ○

ROOM: _____
○ ○ ○ ○ ○ ○ ○

ROOM: _____
○ ○ ○ ○ ○ ○

ROOM: _____
○ ○ ○ ○ ○ ○ ○ ○ ○ ○ ○ ○ ○ ○

ROOM: _____
○ ○ ○ ○ ○ ○ ○ ○ ○

MY BILLS

KEEP TRACK OF YOUR DUE DATES AND BUDGET BY TRACKING YOUR BILLS!

BILL: _____
DUE DATE: _____
AMOUNT DUE: _____
NOTES:
_____
_____

BILL: _____
DUE DATE: _____
AMOUNT DUE: _____
NOTES:
_____
_____

BILL: _____
DUE DATE: _____
AMOUNT DUE: _____
NOTES:
_____
_____

BILL: _____
DUE DATE: _____
AMOUNT DUE: _____
NOTES:
_____
_____

BILL: _____
DUE DATE: _____
AMOUNT DUE: _____
NOTES:
_____
_____

BILL: _____
DUE DATE: _____
AMOUNT DUE: _____
NOTES:
_____
_____

BILL: _____
DUE DATE: _____
AMOUNT DUE: _____
NOTES:
_____
_____

BILL: _____
DUE DATE: _____
AMOUNT DUE: _____
NOTES:
_____
_____

BILL: _____
DUE DATE: _____
AMOUNT DUE: _____
NOTES:
_____
_____

BILL: _____
DUE DATE: _____
AMOUNT DUE: _____
NOTES:
_____
_____

BILL: _____
DUE DATE: _____
AMOUNT DUE: _____
NOTES:
_____
_____

BILL: _____
DUE DATE: _____
AMOUNT DUE: _____
NOTES:
_____
_____

BILL: _____
DUE DATE: _____
AMOUNT DUE: _____
NOTES:
_____
_____

BILL: _____
DUE DATE: _____
AMOUNT DUE: _____
NOTES:
_____
_____

BILL: _____
DUE DATE: _____
AMOUNT DUE: _____
NOTES:
_____
_____

DEBT CHALLENGE

PAY OFF YOUR DEBT AND TRACK YOUR PROGRESS!
SPLIT YOUR DEBT INTO SMALLER AMOUNTS AND FILL IN THE BAGS UNTIL YOU MEET YOUR GOAL!

AMOUNT TO PAY OFF: _____

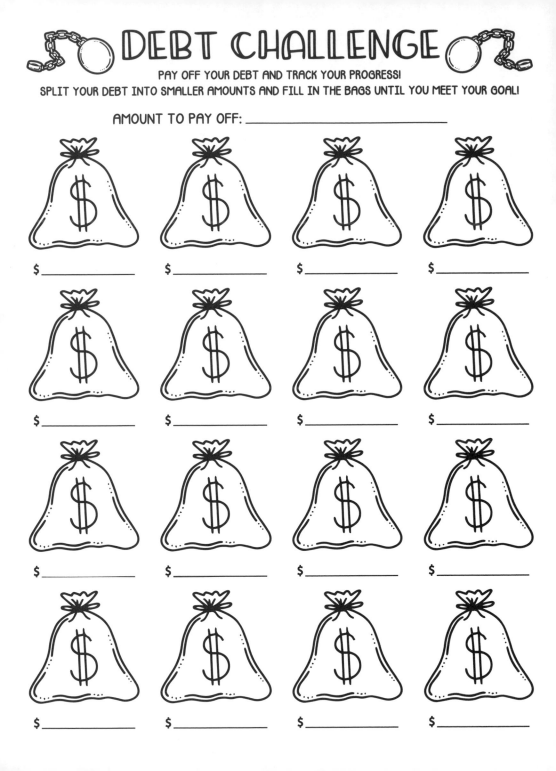

$ _____ $ _____ $ _____ $ _____

$ _____ $ _____ $ _____ $ _____

$ _____ $ _____ $ _____ $ _____

$ _____ $ _____ $ _____ $ _____

MORTGAGE PAYMENT TRACKER

EACH TIME YOU PAY YOUR MORTGAGE, RECORD THE INFORMATION
AND COLOR THE KEY!

PAYMENT:_____
REMAINING:_____
DATE:_____

PAYMENT:_____
REMAINING:_____
DATE:_____

PAYMENT:_____
REMAINING:_____
DATE:_____

PAYMENT:_____
REMAINING:_____
DATE:_____

PAYMENT:_____
REMAINING:_____
DATE:_____

PAYMENT:_____
REMAINING:_____
DATE:_____

PAYMENT:_____
REMAINING:_____
DATE:_____

PAYMENT:_____
REMAINING:_____
DATE:_____

PAYMENT:_____
REMAINING:_____
DATE:_____

PAYMENT:_____
REMAINING:_____
DATE:_____

PAYMENT:_____
REMAINING:_____
DATE:_____

PAYMENT:_____
REMAINING:_____
DATE:_____

TRACKING MY SPENDING

WONDERING WHERE ALL YOUR MONEY WENT? TRACK YOUR SPENDING!

DATE:	ITEM/PURCHASE:	STORE/WEBSITE:	NEED:	WANT:

DATE:	ITEM/PURCHASE:	STORE/WEBSITE:	NEED:	WANT:

ONLINE PURCHASE TRACKER

KEEP TRACK OF ALL YOUR ONLINE PURCHASES!

DATE:	ITEM(S):	STORE/WEBSITE:	DELIVERY DATE:	DELIVERED:
				✓
				✓
				✓
				✓
				✓
				✓
				✓
				✓
				✓
				✓
				✓
				✓
				✓
				✓
				✓
				✓
				✓
				✓
				✓
				✓
				✓
				✓
				✓
				✓
				✓
				✓
				✓
				✓

DATE:	ITEM(S):	STORE/WEBSITE:	DELIVERY DATE:	DELIVERED:
				✓
				✓
				✓
				✓
				✓
				✓
				✓
				✓
				✓
				✓
				✓
				✓
				✓
				✓
				✓
				✓
				✓
				✓
				✓
				✓
				✓
				✓
				✓
				✓
				✓
				✓
				✓

STUDENT LOAN TRACKER

PAY OFF THOSE STUDENT LOANS, AND TRACK YOUR PROGRESS!

PAYMENT:_____
REMAINING:_____
DATE:_____

PAYMENT:_____
REMAINING:_____
DATE:_____

PAYMENT:_____
REMAINING:_____
DATE:_____

PAYMENT:_____
REMAINING:_____
DATE:_____

PAYMENT:_____
REMAINING:_____
DATE:_____

PAYMENT:_____
REMAINING:_____
DATE:_____

PAYMENT:_____
REMAINING:_____
DATE:_____

PAYMENT:_____
REMAINING:_____
DATE:_____

PAYMENT:_____
REMAINING:_____
DATE:_____

PAYMENT:_____
REMAINING:_____
DATE:_____

PAYMENT:_____
REMAINING:_____
DATE:_____

PAYMENT:_____
REMAINING:_____
DATE:_____

PAYMENT:_____
REMAINING:_____
DATE:_____

PAYMENT:_____
REMAINING:_____
DATE:_____

PAYMENT:_____
REMAINING:_____
DATE:_____

PAYMENT:_____
REMAINING:_____
DATE:_____

PAYMENT:_____
REMAINING:_____
DATE:_____

PAYMENT:_____
REMAINING:_____
DATE:_____

PAYMENT:_____
REMAINING:_____
DATE:_____

PAYMENT:_____
REMAINING:_____
DATE:_____

PAYMENT:_____
REMAINING:_____
DATE:_____

PAYMENT:_____
REMAINING:_____
DATE:_____

PAYMENT:_____
REMAINING:_____
DATE:_____

PAYMENT:_____
REMAINING:_____
DATE:_____

PAYMENT:_____
REMAINING:_____
DATE:_____

PAYMENT:_____
REMAINING:_____
DATE:_____

PAYMENT:_____
REMAINING:_____
DATE:_____

PAYMENT:_____
REMAINING:_____
DATE:_____

PAYMENT:_____
REMAINING:_____
DATE:_____

PAYMENT:_____
REMAINING:_____
DATE:_____

PAYMENT:_____
REMAINING:_____
DATE:_____

PAYMENT:_____
REMAINING:_____
DATE:_____

PAYMENT:_____
REMAINING:_____
DATE:_____

SUBSCRIPTION TRACKER

KEEP TRACK OF YOUR ACTIVE SUBSCRIPTIONS!

SUBSCRIPTION:	FREQUENCY:	RENEWAL DATE:	AMOUNT:
	ANNUAL / MONTHLY		
	ANNUAL / MONTHLY		
	ANNUAL / MONTHLY		
	ANNUAL / MONTHLY		
	ANNUAL / MONTHLY		
	ANNUAL / MONTHLY		
	ANNUAL / MONTHLY		
	ANNUAL / MONTHLY		
	ANNUAL / MONTHLY		
	ANNUAL / MONTHLY		
	ANNUAL / MONTHLY		

SUBSCRIPTION:		FREQUENCY:	RENEWAL DATE:	AMOUNT:
		ANNUAL		
		MONTHLY		
		ANNUAL		
		MONTHLY		
		ANNUAL		
		MONTHLY		
		ANNUAL		
		MONTHLY		
		ANNUAL		
		MONTHLY		
		ANNUAL		
		MONTHLY		
		ANNUAL		
		MONTHLY		
		ANNUAL		
		MONTHLY		
		ANNUAL		
		MONTHLY		
		ANNUAL		
		MONTHLY		
		ANNUAL		
		MONTHLY		

SAVINGS TRACKER

FILL THAT PIGGY BANK BY TRACKING YOUR SAVINGS!

AMOUNT: _____
DATE: _____

AMOUNT: _____
DATE: _____

AMOUNT: _____
DATE: _____

AMOUNT: _____
DATE: _____

AMOUNT: _____
DATE: _____

AMOUNT: _____
DATE: _____

AMOUNT: _____
DATE: _____

AMOUNT: _____
DATE: _____

AMOUNT: _____
DATE: _____

AMOUNT: _____
DATE: _____

AMOUNT: _____
DATE: _____

AMOUNT: _____
DATE: _____

AMOUNT: _____
DATE: _____

AMOUNT: _____
DATE: _____

AMOUNT: _____
DATE: _____

AMOUNT: _____
DATE: _____

100 DAYS OF ME TIME

WHETHER IT'S A FULL DAY OR 10 MINUTES A DAY, TAKING TIME FOR YOURSELF IS ESSENTIAL
FOR YOUR MENTAL HEALTH. TRY TO HIT 100 DAYS OF ME TIME!

100 DAYS OF ME TIME

AFTER GETTING YOUR FIRST 100 DAYS OF ME TIME, CAN YOU GET 200 MORE?

POSITIVE SELF-TALK

SOME COMPLIMENTS COME FROM WITHIN. RECORD YOUR POSITIVE SELF-TALK MOMENTS!

HIGHLIGHTS TRACKER

THERE ARE HIGHLIGHTS IN EVERY SINGLE DAY, IF YOU LOOK CAREFULLY ENOUGH.
SHED SOME LIGHT ON THESE SPECIAL MOMENTS!

DATE: _____

DATE: _____

DATE: _____

DATE: _____

DATE: _____

DATE: _____

DATE: _____

DATE: _____

DATE: _____

DATE: _____

DATE: _____

DATE: _____

DATE: _____

DATE: _____

DATE: _____

DATE: _____

DATE: _____

DATE: _____

DATE: _____

DATE: _____

COMPLIMENTS I'VE RECEIVED

GET OUTSIDE

TAKE SOME TIME TO GO OUTDOORS—BREATHE IN THE FRESH AIR, ENJOY NATURE, AND TAKE A BREAK FROM THE STRESS OF THE DAY!

DATE: _____
ACTIVITY: _____
WEATHER: _____
NOTES: _____
_____

DATE: _____
ACTIVITY: _____
WEATHER: _____
NOTES: _____
_____

DATE: _____
ACTIVITY: _____
WEATHER: _____
NOTES: _____
_____

DATE: _____
ACTIVITY: _____
WEATHER: _____
NOTES: _____
_____

DATE: _____
ACTIVITY: _____
WEATHER: _____
NOTES: _____
_____

DATE: _____
ACTIVITY: _____
WEATHER: _____
NOTES: _____
_____

DATE: _____
ACTIVITY: _____
WEATHER: _____
NOTES: _____
_____

DATE: _____
ACTIVITY: _____
WEATHER: _____
NOTES: _____
_____

DATE: _____
ACTIVITY: _____
WEATHER: _____
NOTES: _____
_____

DATE: _____
ACTIVITY: _____
WEATHER: _____
NOTES: _____
_____

MINDFUL MOMENTS

KEEP TRACK OF THOSE SPECIAL TIMES WHEN YOU'RE ABLE TO STAY MINDFUL
AND PRESENT IN THE MOMENT!

MINDFUL MOMENT:

DATE:

DETAILS:

MINDFUL MOMENT:

DATE:

DETAILS:

MINDFUL MOMENT:

DATE:

DETAILS:

MINDFUL MOMENT:

DATE:

DETAILS:

MINDFUL MOMENT:

DATE:

DETAILS:

MINDFUL MOMENT:

DATE:

DETAILS:

MINDFUL MOMENT:

DATE:

DETAILS:

MINDFUL MOMENT:

DATE:

DETAILS:

MINDFUL MOMENT:

DATE:

DETAILS:

MINDFUL MOMENT:

DATE:

DETAILS:

MINDFUL MOMENT:

DATE:

DETAILS:

MINDFUL MOMENT:

DATE:

DETAILS:

MEDITATION TRACKER

EACH DAY YOU MAKE TIME TO PRACTICE MEDITATION, FILL IN A MANDALA!

SMALL VICTORIES

EVEN THE SMALL WINS ARE WORTH CELEBRATING.
RECORD YOUR VICTORIES AND DECORATE YOUR TROPHIES!

VICTORY: _____   VICTORY: _____   VICTORY: _____
_____   _____   _____
DATE: _____   DATE: _____   DATE: _____

VICTORY: _____   VICTORY: _____   VICTORY: _____
DATE: _____   DATE: _____   DATE: _____

VICTORY: _____   VICTORY: _____   VICTORY: _____
DATE: _____   DATE: _____   DATE: _____

VICTORY: _____   VICTORY: _____   VICTORY: _____
_____   _____   _____
DATE: _____   DATE: _____   DATE: _____

VICTORY: _____

DATE: _____

VICTORY: _____

DATE: _____

VICTORY: _____

DATE: _____

VICTORY: _____

DATE: _____

VICTORY: _____

DATE: _____

VICTORY: _____

DATE: _____

VICTORY: _____

DATE: _____

VICTORY: _____

DATE: _____

VICTORY: _____

DATE: _____

VICTORY: _____

DATE: _____

VICTORY: _____

DATE: _____

VICTORY: _____

DATE: _____

JOURNALING TRACKER

TAKING THE TIME TO JOURNAL IS IMPORTANT FOR YOUR MENTAL HEALTH.
EVERY TIME YOU JOURNAL, RECORD THE DATE AND COLOR A NOTEBOOK!

DATE: DATE: DATE: DATE: DATE:

DATE: DATE: DATE: DATE: DATE:

DATE: DATE: DATE: DATE: DATE:

DATE: DATE: DATE: DATE: DATE:

_____   _____   _____   _____   _____

DATE: DATE: DATE: DATE: DATE:

_____   _____   _____   _____   _____

DATE: DATE: DATE: DATE: DATE:

_____   _____   _____   _____   _____

TRIGGER TRACKER

CERTAIN MOMENTS, CONVERSATIONS, AND SITUATIONS CAN TRIGGER ANXIETY OR TRAUMA.
RECORD WHAT TRIGGERS YOU.

HAIR TRACKER

KEEP TRACK OF YOUR LAST APPOINTMENT BY COLORING IN THE
SCISSORS EVERY TIME YOU GET A TRIM OR TREATMENT!

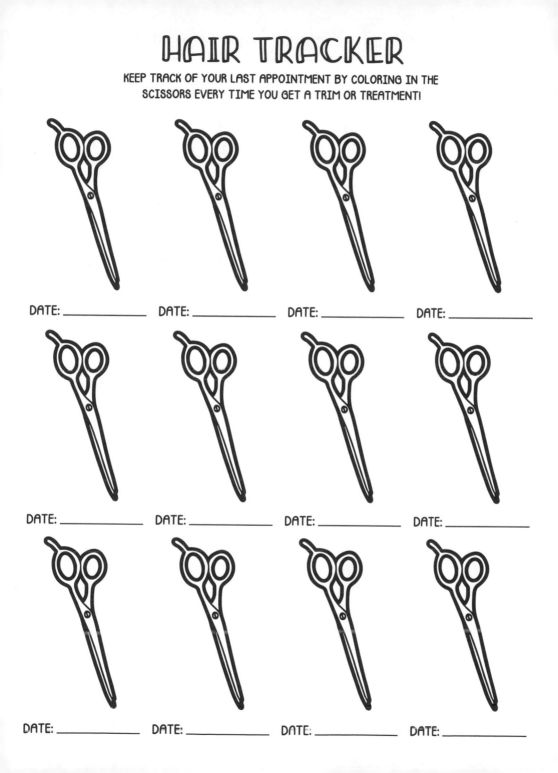

DATE: _____ DATE: _____ DATE: _____ DATE: _____

DATE: _____ DATE: _____ DATE: _____ DATE: _____

DATE: _____ DATE: _____ DATE: _____ DATE: _____

NAIL-CARE TRACKER

KEEP TRACK OF THOSE NAILS! GET A MANI/PEDI? PAINT THEM YOURSELF?
COLOR IN THE BOTTLES BELOW AND ADD THE DATES TO KEEP TRACK!

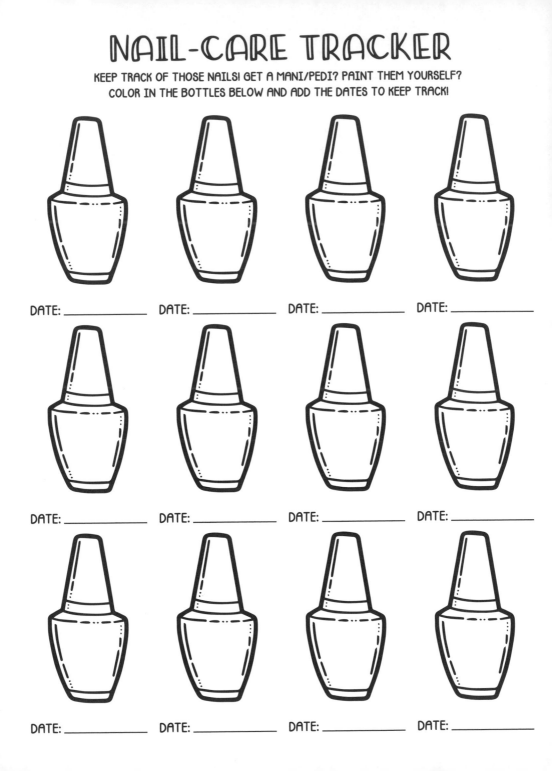

DATE: _____   DATE: _____   DATE: _____   DATE: _____

DATE: _____   DATE: _____   DATE: _____   DATE: _____

DATE: _____   DATE: _____   DATE: _____   DATE: _____

SKINCARE TRACKER

PRODUCT:
_____

PURPOSE:
_____

USAGE:
_____

PRODUCT:
_____

PURPOSE:
_____

USAGE:
_____

PRODUCT:
_____

PURPOSE:
_____

USAGE:
_____

PRODUCT:
_____

PURPOSE:
_____

USAGE:
_____

PRODUCT:
_____

PURPOSE:
_____

USAGE:
_____

PRODUCT:
_____

PURPOSE:
_____

USAGE:
_____

SPA TRACKER

WHETHER AT HOME OR AT THE SPA, KEEP TRACK OF THOSE TREATMENTS!

DATE: _____
TREATMENT(S): _____
_____
COST: _____
NOTES: _____
_____
_____

DATE: _____
TREATMENT(S): _____
_____
COST: _____
NOTES: _____
_____
_____

DATE: _____
TREATMENT(S): _____
_____
COST: _____
NOTES: _____
_____
_____

DATE: _____
TREATMENT(S): _____
_____
COST: _____
NOTES: _____
_____
_____

DATE: _____
TREATMENT(S): _____
_____
COST: _____
NOTES: _____
_____
_____

DATE: _____
TREATMENT(S): _____
_____
COST: _____
NOTES: _____
_____
_____

DATE: _____
TREATMENT(S): _____
_____
COST: _____
NOTES: _____
_____
_____

DATE: _____
TREATMENT(S): _____
_____
COST: _____
NOTES: _____
_____
_____

MORNING ROUTINE

WHAT DOES YOUR IDEAL MORNING LOOK LIKE?
LIST OUT YOUR MORNING ROUTINE, AND CHECK THE STEPS OFF IN PENCIL AS YOU GO!
ERASE THE CHECKMARKS AND REPEAT EACH DAY UNTIL YOUR ROUTINES BECOME HABITS!

- ☐ _____
- ☐ _____
- ☐ _____
- ☐ _____
- ☐ _____
- ☐ _____
- ☐ _____
- ☐ _____
- ☐ _____
- ☐ _____
- ☐ _____
- ☐ _____
- ☐ _____
- ☐ _____
- ☐ _____
- ☐ _____
- ☐ _____
- ☐ _____
- ☐ _____
- ☐ _____

NIGHTTIME ROUTINE

WHAT DOES YOUR IDEAL NIGHT LOOK LIKE?
LIST OUT YOUR NIGHTLY ROUTINE, AND CHECK THE STEPS OFF IN PENCIL AS YOU GO!
ERASE THE CHECKMARKS AND REPEAT EACH DAY UNTIL YOUR ROUTINES BECOME HABITS!

- [ ] _____
- [ ] _____
- [ ] _____
- [ ] _____
- [ ] _____
- [ ] _____
- [ ] _____
- [ ] _____
- [ ] _____
- [ ] _____
- [ ] _____
- [ ] _____
- [ ] _____
- [ ] _____
- [ ] _____
- [ ] _____
- [ ] _____
- [ ] _____
- [ ] _____

BACK UP YOUR WORK

FAR TOO OFTEN, WE FORGET TO BACK UP OUR WORK.
TAKE TIME TO BACK UP THOSE FILES, PHOTOS, AND MORE, THEN RECORD THE DATES!

DATE: _____ DATE: _____ DATE: _____

DATE: _____ DATE: _____ DATE: _____

DATE: _____ DATE: _____ DATE: _____

DATE: _____ DATE: _____ DATE: _____

IDEA TRACKER

KEEP TRACK OF ALL YOUR BRIGHT IDEAS!

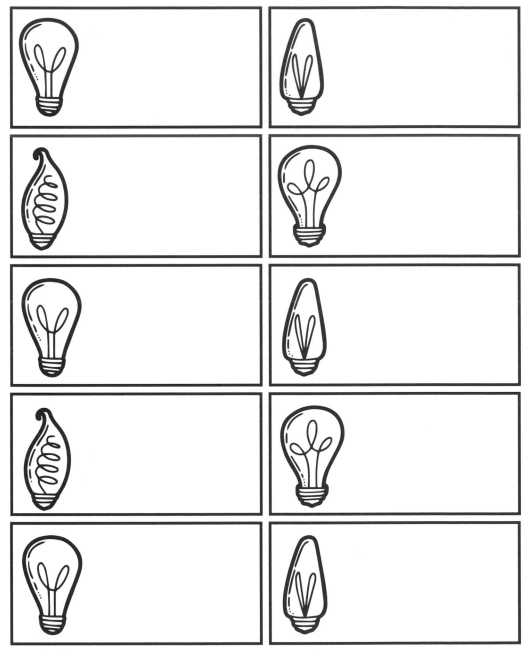

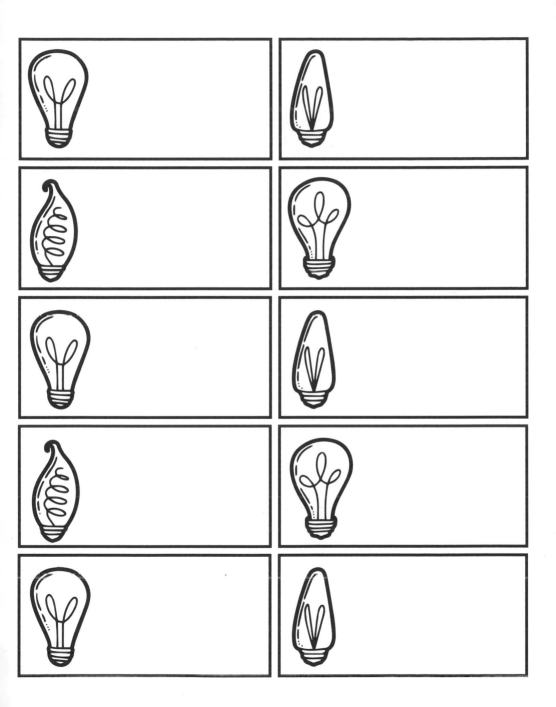

JOB TRACKER

LOOKING FOR A JOB? KEEP TRACK OF YOUR PROSPECTS!

COMPANY:	JOB TITLE:	LOCATION:	SALARY:	CONTACT:	DATE APPLIED:

COMPANY:	JOB TITLE:	LOCATION:	SALARY:	CONTACT:	DATE APPLIED:

PASSWORD TRACKER

KEEP TRACK OF YOUR USERNAMES AND PASSWORDS!
(BE SURE TO KEEP THIS IN A SAFE PLACE.)

WEBSITE/APP:	USERNAME:	PASSWORD:

WEBSITE/APP:	USERNAME:	PASSWORD:

QUESTIONS FOR LATER...

IS CURIOSITY STRIKING YOU, BUT YOU DON'T HAVE THE TIME TO DIVE IN?
TRACK YOUR QUESTIONS NOW AND RECORD YOUR ANSWERS LATER!

QUESTION: _____
_____
ANSWER: _____
_____
_____

QUESTION: _____
_____
ANSWER: _____
_____
_____

QUESTION: _____
_____
ANSWER: _____
_____
_____

QUESTION: _____
_____
ANSWER: _____
_____
_____

QUESTION: _____
_____
ANSWER: _____
_____
_____

QUESTION: _____
_____
ANSWER: _____
_____
_____

QUESTION: _____
_____
ANSWER: _____
_____
_____

QUESTION: _____
_____
ANSWER: _____
_____
_____

QUESTION: _____
_____
ANSWER: _____
_____
_____

QUESTION: _____
_____
ANSWER: _____
_____
_____

QUESTION: _____
_____
ANSWER: _____
_____
_____

QUESTION: _____
_____
ANSWER: _____
_____
_____

THINGS TO LEARN

WE ALL HAVE SO MUCH TO LEARN!
EXPAND YOUR HORIZONS AND LEARN SOMETHING NEW.
TRACK YOUR ENDEAVORS!

TOPIC: _____
TOOLS/RESOURCES NEEDED: _____
_____
NOTES: _____
_____
_____

TOPIC: _____
TOOLS/RESOURCES NEEDED: _____
_____
NOTES: _____
_____
_____

TOPIC: _____
TOOLS/RESOURCES NEEDED: _____
_____
NOTES: _____
_____
_____

TOPIC: _____
TOOLS/RESOURCES NEEDED: _____
_____
NOTES: _____
_____
_____

TOPIC: _____
TOOLS/RESOURCES NEEDED: _____
_____
NOTES: _____
_____
_____

TOPIC: _____
TOOLS/RESOURCES NEEDED: _____
_____
NOTES: _____
_____
_____

TOPIC: _____
TOOLS/RESOURCES NEEDED: _____
_____
NOTES: _____
_____
_____

TOPIC: _____
TOOLS/RESOURCES NEEDED: _____
_____
NOTES: _____
_____
_____

TOPIC: _____
TOOLS/RESOURCES NEEDED: _____
_____
NOTES: _____
_____
_____

TOPIC: _____
TOOLS/RESOURCES NEEDED: _____
_____
NOTES: _____
_____
_____

TOPIC: _____
TOOLS/RESOURCES NEEDED: _____
_____
NOTES: _____
_____
_____

TOPIC: _____
TOOLS/RESOURCES NEEDED: _____
_____
NOTES: _____
_____
_____

TOPIC: _____
TOOLS/RESOURCES NEEDED: _____
_____
NOTES: _____
_____
_____

TOPIC: _____
TOOLS/RESOURCES NEEDED: _____
_____
NOTES: _____
_____
_____

TOPIC: _____
TOOLS/RESOURCES NEEDED: _____
_____
NOTES: _____
_____
_____

TOPIC: _____
TOOLS/RESOURCES NEEDED: _____
_____
NOTES: _____
_____
_____

TOPIC: _____
TOOLS/RESOURCES NEEDED: _____
_____
NOTES: _____
_____
_____

TOPIC: _____
TOOLS/RESOURCES NEEDED: _____
_____
NOTES: _____
_____
_____

TOPIC: _____
TOOLS/RESOURCES NEEDED: _____
_____
NOTES: _____
_____
_____

TOPIC: _____
TOOLS/RESOURCES NEEDED: _____
_____
NOTES: _____
_____
_____

TOPIC: _____
TOOLS/RESOURCES NEEDED: _____
_____
NOTES: _____
_____
_____

TOPIC: _____
TOOLS/RESOURCES NEEDED: _____
_____
NOTES: _____
_____
_____

TOPIC: _____
TOOLS/RESOURCES NEEDED: _____
_____
NOTES: _____
_____
_____

TOPIC: _____
TOOLS/RESOURCES NEEDED: _____
_____
NOTES: _____
_____
_____

NOTES

HEY...THANK YOU!

I'D LIKE TO TAKE THIS OPPORTUNITY TO THANK THOSE WHO HAVE SUPPORTED ME ON THIS JOURNEY...

...MY MOTHER, WHO ALWAYS ENCOURAGED MY CREATIVE AMBITIONS. I'VE HAD THE WONDERFUL PRIVILEGE TO BE RAISED BY A MOTHER WHO SHOWED ME THE IMPORTANCE OF WORKING HARD TOWARD YOUR GOALS. I'D LIKE TO THANK MY DAUGHTER, CHARLOTTE, WHO REMINDS ME DAILY OF THE IMPORTANCE OF BELIEVING IN YOURSELF AND BEING AUTHENTIC TO YOUR CORE.

...MY FRIENDS AND FAMILY FOR THEIR UNWAVERING SUPPORT. SPECIAL THANKS TO THOSE WHO HELD ME UP DURING A VERY DIFFICULT YEAR. YOU KNOW WHO YOU ARE. I'M FOREVER GRATEFUL FOR YOU, AND I COULDN'T HAVE DONE THIS WITHOUT YOU.

...MY @PLANSTHATBLOSSOM FOLLOWING FOR THEIR PATIENCE WHILE I TOOK A BREAK FROM POSTING TO WORK ON THIS BOOK. THEIR KINDNESS AND CREATIVITY INSPIRE ME EVERY SINGLE DAY. I WOULDN'T BE HERE WITHOUT THE ENCOURAGEMENT AND WARMTH OF MY COMMUNITY.

...MY TEACHERS AND MENTORS WHO BUILT ME UP AND BELIEVED IN MY WORK WHEN I FOUND IT DIFFICULT TO DO SO. YOU HELPED SHAPE THE ARTIST I AM TODAY AND SHOWED ME THAT THERE WAS A CREATIVE SPACE FOR ME TO GROW.

...MY WONDERFUL COWORKERS AT PIXITE APPS FOR SUPPORTING MY DREAMS OUTSIDE OF THE WORKPLACE. WORKING ON ZINNIA HAS BEEN THE MOST EXCITING PROFESSIONAL EXPERIENCE, AND I AM SO FORTUNATE TO WORK WITH SO MANY KINDHEARTED AND CREATIVE INDIVIDUALS.

...MY TEAM AT TARCHERPERIGEE/PENGUIN RANDOM HOUSE, ESPECIALLY MY EDITOR, MARIAN LIZZI, FOR GUIDING ME, TEACHING ME, AND BEING COMPASSIONATE AND ENTHUSIASTIC DURING THE PROCESS OF CREATING THIS BOOK.

ABOUT THE AUTHOR

NICOLE BARLETTANO IS AN ILLUSTRATOR WITH AN AFFINITY FOR PLANNING AND JOURNALING. SHE LOVES COMING UP WITH FUN AND FUNCTIONAL PAGES THAT HELP BRING BALANCE AND PRODUCTIVITY TO HERSELF AND OTHERS. SHE'S SHARED HER WORK FOR YEARS WITH HER FOLLOWERS, WHO KNOW HER AS @PLANSTHATBLOSSOM ON INSTAGRAM. SHE IS THE AUTHOR OF <u>MY LIFE IN LISTS</u> AND WORKS FULL TIME AS THE ART DIRECTOR FOR ZINNIA, A JOURNALING AND PLANNING APP BY PIXITE. CREATIVITY AND KINDNESS ARE HER LOVE LANGUAGE...AND CUTE FAT ANIMALS, TOO.

ABOVE ALL, SHE'S A MOTHER TO AN ADORABLE LITTLE GIRL NAMED CHARLOTTE.